Aïda

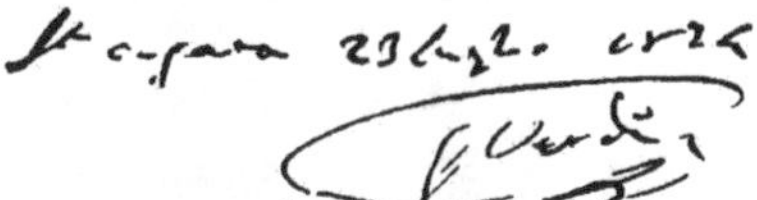
G. Verdi

G. SCHIRMER'S COLLECTION OF OPERAS.

AÏDA

Opera in Four Acts

BY

G. VERDI

LIBRETTO BY

A. GHISLANZONI

THE ENGLISH VERSION BY

MRS. G. G. LAURENCE

WITH AN ESSAY ON THE HISTORY OF THE OPERA BY

W. J. HENDERSON

G. SCHIRMER — NEW YORK.

AÏDA.

FIRST PERFORMED AT CAIRO, EGYPT, DEC. 24, 1871; AND AT MILAN, FEB. 8, 1872.

Characters of the Drama,

With the Original Cast as Presented at the first Performances.

		(At Cairo)	(At Milan)
AÏDA	**Soprano**	**Signora POZZONI**	**Signora STOLZ**
AMNERIS	**Mezzo-soprano**	**Signora GROSSI**	**Signora WALDMANN**
RADAMÈS	**Tenor**	**Signor MONGINI**	**Signor FANCELLI**
AMONASRO	**Baritone**	**Signor STELLER**	**Signor PANDOLFINI**
RAMPHIS	**Bass**	**Signor MEDINI**	**Signor MAINI**
THE KING	**Bass**	**Signor COSTA**	**Signor PAVOLERI**
A MESSENGER	**Tenor**	**Signor BOTTARDI**	**Signor VISTARINI**

Priests, Priestesses, Ministers, Captains, Soldiers, Officials, Ethiopian Slaves and Prisoners, Egyptian Populace, etc.

The scene is in Memphis and Thebes, at the time of the Pharaohs' power.

ACT I.—1. THE KING'S PALACE, AT MEMPHIS; 2. TEMPLE OF VULCAN, AT MEMPHIS. ACT II.—1. A HALL IN THE APARTMENTS OF AMNERIS; 2. BEFORE A GATE OF THE CITY OF THEBES. ACT III.—ON THE BANK OF THE NILE, WITH TEMPLE OF ISIS. ACT IV.—1. HALL IN THE KING'S PALACE; 2. TEMPLE OF VULCAN.

Aïda.

The importance of Verdi's "Aïda" as a work of musical art can hardly be overestimated. It is as certain as anything in art-history can be, that this production revolutionized modern Italian opera, and that to its influence is due the composition of such works as "Cavalleria Rusticana" and "Pagliacci." In itself, the opera marks the beginning of what has been called Verdi's third period. Commentators on his work are fond of pointing out that his style changed when he wrote "Ernani," something more than half a century ago, and that it wholly altered once again, when he produced "Aïda." The change from his first style to his second is one that can be discerned only by very careful students of his scores, but that from his second to his third was at once patent to the entire world. "Aïda" was acclaimed as a revelation of new and unsuspected powers in the composer of

"Il Trovatore" and "La Traviata," though careful judges ought to have said that it was the result of old powers wielded with a new purpose. There was no dissent, however, from the general verdict that the "grand old man" of Italian music had given the world a masterpiece, an opera far and away beyond the best works of Rossini, Donizetti and Bellini, brilliant in its opulence of color, gorgeous in its instrumentation, filled in every measure with a splendor of melodic beauty, and throbbing with dramatic passion. From that verdict there has not yet been any dissent, and the only Italian who has rivaled "Aïda" is Verdi himself in his noble "Otello" and his marvelous "Falstaff."

It is frequently asserted that "Aïda" was written for the opening of the new opera house at Cairo, Egypt, built by Ismail Pacha. The error of this statement, however, is established by the fact that the house was opened in 1869. Ismail Pacha had certain lordly ambitions which did him credit. He desired to appear before the civilized world as a munificent patron of the arts, and his earnest desire was to add to the lustre of his new opera house by producing a work based on an Egyptian story. He naturally turned to Verdi, then the reigning operatic master. Verdi was not at first inclined to accept the offer, and he named as his price a figure so high that he thought it would frighten the Khedive. However, his terms were promptly accepted, and gradually Verdi came to view with interest, and at length with enthusiasm, the opportunities for high coloring and brilliant effects offered by the location of the action in Egypt. The Khedive confided to Mariette Bey, the eminent French Egyptologist, the task of finding a story suitable for operatic treatment and likely to appeal to Verdi. The Bey had found in his studies of ancient Egyptian history an incident from which he developed the original plan of the libretto of "Aïda." This plan was transferred to M. Camille du Locle, who wrote the recitative and lyrics in French prose. His work was done at Verdi's home, at Busseto, Italy, and profited much by the composer's practical advice. Indeed, Verdi did much toward the preparation of his own libretto, and the double stage in the last act, showing Radamès and Aïda dying in the tomb under the temple in which Amneris is bowed in grief, is entirely his. Signor Ghislanzoni translated the French prose into Italian verse, and when the music had been completed, the Italian was translated into French verse for use on the operatic stage of France.

Verdi set to work at once. Meanwhile the Khedive had decided that he would like to have the composer go to Egypt to conduct the first performance. Verdi's price for writing the opera was $20,000, and $30,000 if he went to Egypt. But at the end, his horror of the ocean—he had once gone to London and suffered from sea-sickness—overcame him, and he refused to go at any price. The original plan was to produce the opera toward the close of 1870, and for that purpose the scenery was painted in Paris. But the Franco-Prussian war broke out, and the scenery was a prisoner. Verdi, during the year's postponement, was not idle. He made some important improvements in the score. He cut out a chorus in Palestrina style, and substituted a chorus and a romanza for "Aïda." He had come to the wise conclusion, that the Palestrina style would be incongruous in an Egyptian opera. The opera was produced on December 24, 1871. The conductor was Signor Bottesini, the famous double-bass player, and the cast was as given above. The audience was a strange mixture of Europeans and Orientals. Filippi, the Italian critic, wrote :

"The Arabians, even the rich, do not love our shows; they prefer the mewings of their tunes, the monotonous beatings of their drums, to all the melodies of the past, present, and future. It is a true miracle to see a turban in a theatre of Cairo. Sunday evening the opera house was crowded before the curtain rose. Many of the boxes were filled with women, who neither chattered nor rustled their robes. There was beauty, and there was intelligence, especially among the Greeks and the strangers of rank, who abound in Cairo. For truth's sake, I must add that, by the side of the most beautiful and the most richly dressed, were Coptic and Jewish faces, with strange head-dresses, impossible costumes, a howling of colors,—no one could deliberately have invented worse. The women of the harem could not be seen. They were in the first three boxes on the right, in the second gallery. Thick white muslin hid their faces from prying glances."

The success of the opera was most emphatic. A chorus of praise rang through Europe, and the genius of Verdi was acclaimed in glowing terms. "Aïda" was next given at La Scala, Milan, February 8, 1872. It was given in Paris on April 22, 1876, with Mme. Stolz, Mlle. Waldmann, Signor Masini, Signor Pandolfini, Signor Medini, and M. Edouard de Reszké in the cast. The first performance in America was given at the Academy of Music, New York, on November 26, 1873, with the following great cast: Aïda, Octavia Torriani; Amneris, Annie Louise Cary; Radamès, Signor Italo Campanini; Amonasro, M. Victor Maurel; Ramphis, Signor Nannetti; King, Signor Scolara.

The story of "Aïda" is supposed to belong to the time of the Pharaohs, and its action is located at Memphis and Thebes. The first act begins in the King's palace in the former city. The High Priest, Ramphis, tells Radamès that the Ethiopians are marching against Egypt and that the goddess Isis has named the leader of the defending army. Radamès, left alone, declares how happy he would be could he lead the army to victory and return to lay his laurels at the feet of Amneris's slave, Aïda, whom he loves. Amneris and Aïda join him. Amneris loves him, and from his demeanor and that of Aïda she suspects the truth. She swears to avenge herself if her suspicion proves correct. The King and his court enter, and presently a messenger comes to announce that it is Amonasro who is leading the invaders. Amonasro is Aïda's father, but she alone knows this. The King declares that Isis has chosen Radamès to lead the Egyptian army, and directs him to go to the temple of Ftha (Ptah) to receive the consecrated arms. The scene concludes with a martial ensemble. The second scene takes place in the temple, where the priests invoke Ftha and the priestesses dance the sacred dance. Radamès receives the arms, and departs upon his mission.

The second act opens in the apartments of Amneris at Thebes. Amneris bewails the absence of Radamès, and her slaves vainly try to console her. Aïda enters, and Amneris, to test her, says that news has come of the death of Radamès.

Aïda's grief betrays her love, and Amneris threatens her with destruction. The second scene shows a great square, into which the triumphal army marches with Radamès glorified as a conqueror. He brings with him a number of Ethiopian prisoners, among them Amonasro, who is not known to be the king. Aïda rushes to her father's arms, and joins him in begging for the lives of the prisoners. Radamès, seeing Aïda's grief, joins in the prayer, which Amneris and the priests oppose. The King releases all the prisoners save Amonasro, who is to remain as a slave with Aïda. Then, to the joy of Amneris, and the horror of Radamès and Aïda, the King bestows his daughter's hand on Radamès.

The third act takes place on the Nile's bank before the temple of Isis, whither Amneris, on the eve of marriage, has gone to pray. Aïda has made an appointment to meet Radamès near the temple, and while she waits for him she bewails her separation from her native land. She is surprised by her father, who has discovered her love for Radamès, and orders her to induce the young man to reveal the plans of the Egyptians. Aïda at first refuses, but after an outburst of savage wrath on the part of her father, she consents. Radamès arrives. Amonasro conceals himself. Aïda tries to lure Radamès to flight with her. He yields, and discloses the Egyptian plans. Amonasro appears, announces that he has overheard, and that he is the king of Ethiopia. Amneris comes out of the temple in time to overhear some of the dialogue. Amonasro rushes upon her with his knife. Radamès interferes and forces Amonasro and Aïda to fly, while he remains and surrenders himself to Ramphis.

The fourth act opens in a chamber adjoining the court in which Radamès is to be tried. Radamès is brought in for trial, and is met by Amneris. She beseeches him to abandon Aïda, and promises that she will intercede for him if he will do so. He refuses. She tells him that Amonasro has been killed and that Aïda has fled. Still he refuses, and Amneris bitterly repents the outcome of her own jealousy. The priests lead Radamès to trial. Amneris, in an agony of grief, hears them accuse him, while he submits in silence to condemnation. They return with their prisoner, and as they pass out Amneris curses them. The second scene shows the temple and the vault beneath it. Radamès, shut in the vault, breathes a prayer that Aïda may never know his fate. But Aïda, who has already found her way to the vault and awaited him there, comes forward. They embrace one another, while above the priestesses sing their chant. Aïda dies in the arms of Radamès, while Amneris, garbed in mourning robe, enters the temple and sinks prostrate in despair upon the huge stone that closes the vault.

This is an admirable story for operatic treatment. It presents an effective sequence of the grand emotions—love, joy, hatred, jealousy, despair and rage, all of which are susceptible of adequate musical expression. It offers a fine variety of action and scenery, and excellent opportunity for spectacular display. The glitter and pomp of the triumphal procession at the close of the second act make a strong and impressive contrast with the subdued glory of the moonlight night on the banks of the Nile in the third act. Indeed, there are few operas in which the scenic surroundings, the action and the emotions are so completely in accord, and it is partly owing to this that Verdi was able to make his music a puissant element in a powerful organization. As for the music, it is difficult to speak of it without appearing to indulge in extravagant praise. It is so rich in melody and harmony, so closely wedded in expressive power to the meaning of the text and so broadly dramatic in all its aspects, that it claims a place among the most striking art-products of our time. The glitter of theatrical tinsel offends finer taste here and there, but, as a whole, "Aïda" is without doubt a masterpiece.

It is an opera from which one can easily select "gems," but closer study will convince the music-lover that it is a necklace of equally fine jewels. The opening recitation of Ramphis and Radamès, by its melodious character and the strong coloring of its accompaniment, invites one to enter at once the enchanted domain of the ancient East. The first aria of Radamès, "Celeste Aïda," is full of character and tenderness, and in the ensuing trio the note of tragic portent is firmly sounded. The martial finale makes the first scene a sort of prologue to the opera, summing up, as it does with its pomp of war, the opening chapter of love, jealousy, ambition and defiance. All the passions of the drama make their appearance in elementary form in the first scene, and give us a foretaste of what is to come. The dance and song of the priestesses in the temple of Ftha are weirdly Oriental in character, and the invocation is broad and dignified. The opening of the scene in the chamber of Amneris is luxurious in color and feeling, while the duet between the princess and her slave is full of passion. The finale of the act, the triumphal procession and the plea for the prisoners, is dazzling in its splendor.

But Verdi reaches his climax in the Nile scene. In all Italian opera there is no finer example of the true aria than Aïda's "O patria mia." It is eloquent in its expressive power, beautiful in its pure melody, perfect in form, and subtly forceful in its harmonization. The subsequent duet for Aïda and Amonasro is a superb piece of writing, while the duet for Aïda and Amneris, though it falls somewhat more into the habit of theatrical diction, especially in its *ad captandum* close, has nevertheless the power of a warm mood-picture. The remainder of the opera is less effective with the general audience, but it is all good music and beautiful.

Those who are familiar with Verdi's earlier works, such as "La Traviata" and "Il Trovatore," while they may detect in "Aïda" occasional reminiscences of them, cannot fail to perceive the great change in the master's style. In "Aïda" he has abandoned the elementary dance-rhythms, the antique melodic formulæ, the bald and empty passages of recitative between the set numbers, and the cheap and noisy instrumentation. The rhythms are broader and more scholarly; the melody is fresh, original and diversified in character; the harmony is immensely rich and expressive, and the instrumentation glows with Oriental warmth of color. The critics who went to Cairo in 1871 declared that Verdi, the Italian Verdi of the honey-tuned Neapolitan school of composers, had been inoculated with the virus of Wagnerism. It would have been strange, indeed, if Verdi had not discerned the general trend of operatic art under the stimulus of Wagner's proclamations; but although he arose and girded himself to step to the place rightly his in the van of progress, he made no sacrifices of his own individuality.

Verdi remained in "Aïda" as truly an Italian composer as he was in "Rigoletto." His melody was purely Italian in its technical character and its adherence to the fundamental forms of its school. He continued to employ the set forms, the aria, duet, trio, etc., but he molded them on broader lines and infused into them a truer dramatic utterance. He remodeled his instrumentation so as to add to his operatic canvas all the colors of the modern orchestral palette. In a word, he showed how a man of genius could vitalize the shopworn apparatus of Italian grand opera, just as Mozart had done nearly a century earlier in his "Don Giovanni." In his earlier works Verdi demonstrated that he possessed immense vigor, abundant melodic invention, and inexhaustible resourcefulness. But he was working on the lines of tradition, and the traditions of the Neapolitan school, founded by Alessandro Scarlatti, father of the operatic aria, and maintained by Rossini, Donizetti and Bellini, demanded tunefulness for its own sake without regard to the spirit of the text. It was when Verdi threw overboard the traditions of this school and adapted its methods, after modernizing them, to the legitimate business of dramatic expression, that he produced "Aïda," a work which ought to live among the masterpieces of our era.

Some critics have affected to discover "leading motives" of the Wagnerian kind in "Aïda," but such critics do not understand the nature of the Wagner system. Verdi does use a melodic phrase to indicate the personality of Aïda, but it is employed chiefly to herald her entrance. Other commentators have pointed to his instrumentation as an evidence that he had succumbed to the influence of Wagner. But in "Aïda" Verdi for the first time in his career made a deliberate attempt at local color. Some writers have pointed out what they believed to be Oriental themes in his music. Whether he adapted extant themes to his purpose or not is a matter of small import. The main point is that he employed a scheme of harmony and instrumental color which keeps the Oriental locale of the opera constantly in the hearer's mind. The music of "Aïda" is fitted not only to the emotions of the drama, but to the scene of action, and that, too, without any clap-trap obtrusiveness.

The career of Verdi is an epitome of the history of Italian opera in his time, for he has been the leader of his school. His followers number all the members of what has been called the young Italian school. Its one product has been the condensed opera, such as "Pagliacci." The one-act operas of Mascagni and Leoncavallo employ every item of Verdi's apparatus as found in "Aïda." The single new element is the condensation. Verdi has been the model and the despair of these younger men. Whosoever desires to know the Italian opera of our time at its best, should study the scores of Verdi's last three operas, "Aïda," "Otello" and "Falstaff." But of these three, the first is the only one that preserves the forms of the older school, and hence it is to-day and must remain for all time the noblest example of Italian opera as established by its most admirable exponents.

W. J. Henderson.

Index.

AÏDA.

Opera in Four Acts
by
G. VERDI.

Prelude.

Andante mosso. (♩ = 76)

ppp
m.d.
pp
cresc.
ff
dolciss.
dolce

mf
f
incalzando e cresc.
cresc. molto
fff
dim.
ppp
pppp
ppp
pp
morendo
8

Act I.

Introduction.

SCENE I. Hall in the palace of the King at Memphis. To the right and left, a colonnade with statues and flowering shrubs. At the back a grand gate, from which may be seen the temples and palaces of Memphis, and the Pyramids.

Allegro assai moderato. (♩ = 92.)

(Radamès and Ramphis in consultation.)

Ramphis.
Piano.
Sì: corre voce che l'Etiope ardisca sfidarci ancora, e del Nilo la valle e Tebe minacciar. Fra breve un messo recherà il ver.
Yes, it is rumored that the Ethiop dares once again our power, and the valley of Nilus threatens, and Thebes as well. The truth from messengers I soon shall learn.
p legato
Radamès.
La sacra Iside consultasti?
Hast thou consulted the will of Isis?
p

Ramphis.
El-la ha no-ma-to del l'E-gi-zie fa-lan-gi il con-dot-
She hath de-clar-ed who of E-gypt's re-nown-ed ar-mies
Radamès.
Oh lui fe-li-ce!
Oh hap-py mor-tal!
Ramphis.
tier su-pre-mo.
shall be lead-er.
pp
Ramphis. (Looking significantly at Radamès.)
Gio-va-ne e pro-de è des-so.
Young in years is he, and dauntless.
O-ra, del Nu-me re-co i de-cre-ti al
The dread com-mand-ment I to the King shall
(exit.)
Re.
take.
dim. sempre
morendo

Romance.

Recitative.
Radamès.
Piano.
Se quel guerrier io fos-si! se il mio so-gno si av-ve-ras-se!
What if 'tis I am chosen, and my dream be now ac-complish'd!
Allegro vivo. (♩ = 126.)
con entusiasmo
Un e-ser-ci-to di
Of a glorious ar-my
pro-di da me gui-da-to
I the cho-sen lea-der,
e la vit-
mine glorious
to-ria
vict'-ry,
e il plau-so di Men-fi tut-ta!
by Mem-phis re-ceiv'd in tri-umph!
E a te, mia dol-ce A-i-da, tor-nar di lau-ri
To thee re-turn'd, A-i-da, my brow entwin'd with
ff
p

cin - to dir - ti: per te ho pu - gna - to, per te ho
lau - rel: tell thee, for thee I bat - tled, for thee I
f
vin - to!
conquer'd!
ff
pp
Andantino. (♪ = 116.)
con espress.
Ce - le - ste A - i - da, for - ma di -
Heav'n - ly A - i - da, beau - ty re -
p
m.s.
vi - na, mi - sti - co ser - to di lu - ce e
splen - dent, Ra - di - ant flow - er, bloom - ing and
dolce
pp
m.s.

fior, del mio pen-
bright; Queen - ly thou
8
portate la voce
sie - ro tu sei re - gi - na, tu di mia
reign - est o'er me trans - cen - dent, Bathing my
24
ten.
m.s.
vi - ta sei lo splen - dor.
spir-it in beau - ty's light.
p espress.
m.s.
sempre dolciss.
Il tuo bel cie - lo vor - rei ri - dar - ti, le dol - ci
Would that, thy bright skies once more be - hold-ing, Breathing the
m.d.
m.s.
m.d.
m.s.

animando un poco
brez-ze del pa-trio suol: un re-gal ser - to sul crin po -
air of thy na-tive land, Round thy fair brow a di - a - dem
ten.
m.d.
con entusiasmo
sar - - ti, er - ger - ti un tro - - no vi - ci - no al
fold - - ing, Thine were a throne by the sun to
f
f
col canto
sol, ah! Ce - le - ste A -
stand, ah! Heav'n - ly A -
p leggerissime
espress.
i - da, for - ma di - vi - na,
i - da, beau - ty re - splen - dent,

pp
mi - sti - co rag - gio di lu - ce e
Ra - di - ant flow - er, bloom - ing and
fior, del mio pen - sie - ro
bright, Queen - ly thou reign - est
p
tu sei re - gi - na, tu di mia
o'er me trans - cen - dent, Bath - ing my
vi - ta sei lo splen - dor.
spir - it in beau - ty's light.
p

parlante ppp
Il tuo bel cie - lo vor-rei ri-dar-ti, le dol - ci brez - ze del pa-trio
Would that, thy bright skies once more be-hold-ing, Breathing the airs of thy na-tive
ancora p
animando
suol; un re - gal ser - to sul crin po - sar - ti, er - ger-ti un
land, Round thy fair brow a di - a - dem fold - ing, Thine were a
ancora p
pppp
ppp
dim.
tro - no vi - ci-no al sol, un tro - no vi - ci-no al
throne by the sun to stand, a throne by the sun to
ppp
pp leggermente
morendo
pp
sol, un tro - no vi - ci-no al sol.
stand, a throne by the sun to stand.
p
ppp
allarg. e morendo

Duet.

Amneris and Radamès.

Terzet.

Aïda, Amneris & Radamès.

stent.
f
spet-to tan-ta lu - ce di gau - dio in te de-stas - se!
presence could have pow - er to kin-dle in thee such rap - ture!
stent.
pp
Radamès. Recit.
Allegro. (𝅗𝅥 = 100)
D'un so-gno av-ven- tu - ro-so si be-a-va il mio co - - re.
A dream of proud am - bi-tion in my heart I was nurs - ing:
Recit.
p
Recit.
Og - gi, la Di-va proffer-se il no-me del guer-rier che al cam-po le schie-re e-
I - sis this day has declar'd by name the warrior-chief ap-point-ed to lead to
gi - zie con-dur - rà Ah! s'io fos-si a tal o - nor pre-
bat-tle E-gypt's host! Ah! for this hon-or, say, what if I were
f

Andante mosso (♩ = 84)
Amneris.
grazioso
scel-to...
cho-sen?
Nè un al-tro so-gno ma-
Has not an-oth-er vi-
a tempo
p dolciss.
Più lento (♩ = 66)
rall.
con espansione
i più gen-til, più so-a-ve, al co-re ti par-lò? Non hai tu in
sion, one more sweet, more en-chanting, found fa-vor in your heart? Hast thou in
col canto
f
Radamès.
(sotto voce)
(aside)
Men-fi de-si-de-rii... spe-ran-ze? I-o! (quale in-
Memphis no at-trac-tion... more charming? I! (fa-tal
dim.
ppp
Allegro agitato e presto. (𝅗𝅥 = 132)
chie-sta!)
question!)
(Forse...
(Has she...
far-ca-no a-
the se-cret
pp

mo - re
yearning
sco - prì
Di - vin'd
che m'ar - de in
with - in me
Amneris. (aside)
co - re_)
burning?)
(Oh guai!
(Ah me!
se un al - tro a-
my love if
mo - re
spurning
ar - des - se a lu - i nel
His heart to an - oth - er were
Radamès.
co - re!)
turning!)
Del - la sua schia - va il no - me
Have then mine eyes be - tray'd me,
mi les - se nel pen-
And told A - i - da's

Amneris.
Guai se il mi - o sguar - do pe - ne-tra que - sto fa-tal mi-
Woe if hope should false have play'd me, And all in vain my
sier!
name!
ster! gua - i se il mi - o sguar - do pe - ne-tra que-sto fa-tal mi-
flame! Ah, woe if hope should false have play'd me, And all in vain my
For - se mi les - se nel pen -
Have then mine eyes told A - i - da's
f
ster! gua - i se il mi - o sguar - do pe - ne-tra que-sto fa-tal mi-
flame! Ah, woe if hope should false have play'd me, And all in vain my
ster! For - se mi les - se, mi les - se nel pen-
name? Have then mine eyes told, yes, told A - i - da's
f

p
ster! oh! gua-i, oh! gua-i, oh, gua-i!)
flame! ah! woe, ah! woe, ah! woe!)
p
sier, mi les - se nel pen-sier!)
name, have told A - i - da's name!)
p
rall.
Andante mosso. (♩ = 76.)
(enter Aïda)
p dolce espress.
pp
Radamès.
(seeing Aïda)
Amneris.
(aside)
(watching)
Des - sa! (Ei si tur-ba e qua - le
She here! (He is troubled Ah, what a
Allegro. Tempo I.
sguar-do ri-vol - se a lei! A - i-da!
gaze doth he turn on her! A - i-da!
dolce
p cresc.

a me ri - va - le! for - - - - - - se sa -
Have I a ri - val? Can it be
Andante mosso. (♩=76.)
(turning to Aïda.)
con grazia
ria co - stei?) Vie - ni, o di - let - ta, appress - sa - ti
she her - self?) Come hith - er, thou I dear - ly prize
pp
schia - va non sei nè an - cel - la qui do - ve in dol - ce fa - sci - no
Slave art thou none, nor me - nial; Here have I made by fond - est ties
io ti chia - mai so - rel - la. Pian - gi? del - le tue
Sis - ter a name more ge - nial. Weep'st thou? Oh tell me
p
pp

Aïda.
Più mosso.
Ohimè! di guerra
A-las! the cry of
la - cri-me sve-la il se - gre - to, sve - la il se-gre-to a me.
where-fore thou ev - er art mourning, where-fore thy tears now flow.
Più mosso. (♩=112.)
mf
fre - mere l'a - tro - ce gri-di io sen - to Per l'in-fe-li - ce
war I hear, Vast hosts I see as - sem - ble There-fore the coun-try's
Amneris.
pa - tri-a, per me, per voi pa-ven - to. Fa-vel-li il ver? nè
fate I fear, For me, for all I trem-ble. And art thou sure no
rall.
pp
(Aïda casts down her eyes and tries to hide her emotion.) Allegro come prima.
s'a-gi - ta più gra - ve cu - ra in te?
deep-er woe now bids thy tears to flow?
pp

Amneris. (aside, regarding Aïda.)
con voce cupa
(Trema! o re - a schiava!
(Tremble! oh thou base vassal!
Radamès. (aside, regarding Amneris.)
(Nel
(Her
Ah!
Yes!
vol- - - -to a lei ba - le - na_
glance with an - ger flashing_
trema, rea schia - va, trema,
tremble, base vas - sal, tremble,
lo sde - gno ed il so-
Proclaims our love sus-

ch'io nel tu - o cor di-scen-da!
Lest, thy se - cret stain de-tect-ed,
spet-to
pect-ed
guai se l'ar-ca-no af-
Woe! if my hopes all
f
Tre - ma che il ver m'ap -
All in vain thou wouldst dis -
fet - to a noi leg-ges-se in co - re!
dash-ing She mar the plans I've laid!
f
Aïda.
(Aside.) Cantabile.
(Ah!
(No!
pren - da quel pian - to e quel ros - sor!
sem - ble, By tear and blush be - trayed!
guai se leg-ges - se in cor! Nel vol - to a
Woe if she mar my plans! Her glanc - es with
Cantabile.
pp

no, sul - - la mia pa - -
fate, o'er E - gypt loom -
Rea schia - va, 'tre-ma ch'io
Oh thou base vas-sal, tremble lest
lei ba-le - - na
rage are flash - ing,
tria non ge - -
ing, Weighs down
nel tuo cor di-
thy love be de-
lo sde - - gno
Pro - claim - - ing

me il cor, il cor sol - tan - to;
on my heart, my heart de - ject - ed,
scen - - da.
ah
tect - - ed.
Thou
ed il so - spet - to.
our love sus - pect - ed.
quel - - - lo
I wept
tre - ma che il ver,
ah
wouldst all in vain,
thou
guai se l'ar - ca - no af - fet - to,
Woe, if my hopes all dash - ing,

ch'io ver - - - - so è pian - -
that love thus was doom - -
tre - ma che il ver m'ap-
wouldst all in vain dis-
guai se l'ar - ca - no af - fet - to
Woe, if my hopes all dashing
to, è pian - - - -
ing, was doom - - - -
pren - da, ah tre - -
sem - ble, yes, thou
a noi leg - gesse in cor!
She mar the plans I've laid!

to, pian - - to di sven - -
ing, doom - - ing to woe
ma che il ver m'ap - pren - da quel
wouldst all in vain dis - sem - ble, by
guai se l'ar - ca - no af - fet - to a
Ah woe! if my hopes all dash - ing She
- - tu - ra - - - - - - to a - mor!
a hap - - - - - less maid!
pian - to e quel ros - sor! ah
tear and by blush be - trayed! ah
noi leg - ges - se, leg - ges - se in cor!
mar the plans, mar the plans I've laid!

ah! è pian
wept! that love
tre - ma che il ver, ah tre -
trem - ble, vas - sal base, Lest thy
guai se l'ar - ca - no af - fet
Woe if my hopes all dash
to, pian - to di sven
was doom - ing to woe
ma che il ver m'ap - pren - da quel
se - cret be - de - tect - ed, By
to, guai se l'ar - ca - no af - fet - to a
ing, ah me, if my hopes dash - ing She

- - tu - ra - - - - - to a - mor!
— a hap - - - - less maid!
pian - to e quel ros - sor! tre -
tear and by blush be - tray'd! thy
noi leg - ges - se, leg - ges - se in cor!
mar the plans, mar the plans I've laid!
pian - - - - - to
doom - - - - - ing
ma che il ver m'ap - pren - - da quel pian - to, quel
se - cret be de - tect - - ed, By tear and
ah guai se a noi leg - ges - se in cor! oh guai se a
Woe, if she mar the plans I have laid! Woe, if she

di sven-tu - ra - - to a - mor, è pian-to di
to woe a hap - less maid, was dooming to
pian - to e quel ros - sor, tre - ma o schia - va,
blush, and blush be - trayed! Trem - ble, vas - sal,
no - i leg - ges - se in cor, oh guai a no-i- oh
mar the plans I have laid, ah, woe if she should
sventu - ra - - - - - to a - mor!)
woe a hap - - - - - less maid!)
tre - ma o schia - - va, ah! tre - - - ma.)
trem - ble, vas - - sal, ah! trem - - - ble.)
guai, guai se a noi leg - ges - - se in cor!)
mar, mar, should mar the plans I've laid!)
f
ff

Scene and Concerted Piece.

(The King, preceded by his guards and followed by Ramphis, his Ministers, Priests, Captains, etc., etc.; an officer of the Palace, and afterwards a messenger.)

Allegro sostenuto. (♩=116.)
Piano.
f
tr
The King.
Al-ta cagion v'a-duna,o fi-di E-gizii,al vostro Re d'in-tor-no.
Mighty the cause that summons round their King the faithful sons of E-gypt.
pp stacc.

Dai con-fin d'E - tiò-pia un Mes - sag - gie - ro dian - zi giun - ge - a.
From the E - thiop's land a mes - sen - ger this mo - ment has reach'd us.
Gra - vi no - vel - le ei re - ca.
Ti - dings of im - port brings he.
Vi piac-cia u - dir - lo.
Be pleas'd to hear him.
(to an officer.)
Più lento. (♩ = 80.)
Il Mes-sag-gier s'a - van-zi!
Now let the man come forward!
pp con espress.
pppp
Messenger.
Il sa - cro suo - lo del - l'E - git - to è in - va - so dai bar - ba - ri E -
The sa - cred lim - its of E - gyp - tian soil are by E - thiops in -
incalz. a poco a poco
tio - pi.
i no - stri cam - pi fur de - va - sta - ti. ar - se le
vad - ed.
Our fer - tile fields lie all de - vas - tat - ed. de - stroy'd our
f incalz. a poco a poco

mes - si — e bal - di del - la fa - cil vit - to - ria, i pre - da -
har - vest — Embolden'd by so ea - sy a con - quest, the plun-d'ring
Radamès.
Allegro.
Ed o - san tan - to!
Presumptuous daring!
Messenger.
to - ri già marcia - no su Te - be. —
horde on the Cap - i - tal are marching. —
Un guerrie - ro in - do -
They are led by a
The King.
Ed o - san tan - to!
Presumptuous daring!
Ramphis.
Ed o - san tan - to!
Presumptuous daring!
TENOR.
Chorus of Priests.
BASS.
Ed o - san tan - to!
Presumptuous dar - ing!
TENOR.
Chorus of Ministers and Captains.
BASS.
Ed o - san tan - to!
Presumptuous dar - ing!
Allegro. (♩ = 138.)

Aïda.
(aside)
(Mio
(My
Radamès.
Il Re!
The King!
Messenger.
ma - bi - le, fe - ro - ce, li con - du - ce, A - mo - na - sro.
war - rior, un-daunted, nev - er con-quer'd: A - mo - na - sro.
The King.
Il Re!
The King!
Ramphis.
Il Re!
The King!
Il Re!
The King!
Il Re!
The King!
Il Re!
The King!
Il Re!
The King!
pp
Aïda.
pa - dre!)
fa - ther!)
Messenger.
Già Te - bе è in ar - mi e dal - le cen - to por - te sul bar - baro in - va -
All Thebes has ris - en, and from her hundred portals has pour'd on the in -
pp

so re pro - rom - pe - rà, guer - ra re - can - do e
vad - er a tor - rent fierce, fraught with re - lent - less
mor - te.
car - nage.
The King.
a tempo
Sì: guer - ra e mor - te il no - stro gri - do
Ay, death and bat - tle be our ral - lying
a tempo
Radamès.
Guerra!
Bat-tle!
The King.
si-a!
cry!
Ramphis.
Guerra!
Bat-tle!
guerra!
bat-tle!
TENOR.
Chorus of Priests
BASS.
Guerra!
Bat-tle!
guerra!
bat-tle!
TENOR.
Chorus of Ministers and Captains.
BASS.
Guerra!
Bat-tle!
guerra!
bat-tle!
cresc.

Radamès.
guerra! tremen - da, i - ne - so -
bat-tle! and car - nage, war un - re -
Ramphis.
guerra! tremen - da, i - ne - so -
bat-tle! and car - nage, war un - re -
guerra! guerra! tremen - da, i - ne - so -
bat-tle! bat-tle! and car - nage, war un - re -
guerra! guerra! tremen - da, i - ne - so -
bat-tle! bat-tle! and car - nage, war un - re -
guerra!
bat-tle!
ff
Radamès.
ra - ta. (addressing Radamès.)
lenting! Recit.
The King.
I - si - de ve - ne - ra - ta di nos - tre schie - re in - vit - te già de - si -
I - sis, re - ve - red God - dess, al - read - y has ap - point - ed the warrior -
Ramphis.
ra - ta.
lenting!
ra - ta.
lent - ing!
ra - ta.
lent - ing!
p

Aïda.
Ra - da - mès!
Ra - da - mès!
Amneris.
Ra - da - mès!
Ra - da - mès!
The King.
gna - vail con - dot - tier su - pre - mo: Ra - da - mès!
chief with pow'r supreme in - vest - ed. Ra - da - mès!
TENOR.
Ra - da - mès!
Ra - da - mès!
Chorus of Ministers and Captains.
BASS.
Ra - da - mès!
Ra - da - mès!
ppp
(Io tre - mo,
(I trem - ble,
ppp
(Ei du - ce!
Our lea - der,
ff
Radamès.
Ah! sien gra - zie ai Nu - mi! son
Ah! ye Gods, I thank you! My
Ra - da - mès!
Ra - da - mès!
ppp
Ra - da -
Ra - da -
ff
pp

io tre-mo.)
I tremble.)
ei du-ce!)
our leader!)
pa-ghi i vo-ti miei!
dear-est wish is crown'd!
The King.
Or, di Vul-ca-no al tempio muo-vi, o guer-
Now un-to Vulcan's temple, chief-tain, pro-
mes!
mes!
Ra-damès!
Ra-damès!
ppp
Ra-da-mès!
Ra-da-mès!
p
rier; le sa-cre armi ti cin-gi e alla vit-to-ria vo-la.
ceed, there to gird thee to vict-'ry, don-ning sa-cred ar-mor.
ff
Allegro maestoso. (♩= 88.)
marc. assai
Su! del Ni-lo al sa-cro li-do ac-cor-re-te, E-gi-zii e-
On! of Ni-lus' sa-cred riv-er Guard the shores, E-gyp-tians
mf

roi, da o-gni cor pro-rom-pa il grido: guerra e mor-te,_ morte allo stra-
brave, Un-to death the foe de - liv-er, Egypt they nev-er,_ never shall en-
Ramphis.
nier! Glo-ria ai Nu - mi! o-gnun ram-men - ti ch'es - si_
slave! Glo - ry ren-der, glo - ry a - bid - ing, To our_
reg - go - no gli e - ven - ti, che in po - ter d'e Numi so - lo stan le
Gods, the_war-rior guiding; In their pow'r on - ly con - fid - ing, Their pro -
The King.
Su! su! del
On, on! of
sor - ti_ del guer - rier, o - gnun_ ram -
tec - tion_ let us crave, the war - rior_
TENOR.
Chorus
of Min. and Cap.
BASS.
Su! del Ni - lo al sa - cro_
On! of Ni - lus' sa - cred_
Su! del Ni - lo al sa - cro_
On! of Ni - lus' sa - cred_

Ni - lo al sa - cro li - do ac - cor - re - te, E - gi - zi i e - ro - i.
Ni - lus' sa-cred riv-er Guard the shores, E-gyptians brave;
men - ti che in po - ter dei Nu - mi,
guiding, in their pow'r con - fid - ing,
li - do sien bar - rie - ra i no - stri pet - ti; non ec -
riv - er Guard the shores, E - gyp - tians brave, Un - to
li - do sien bar - rie - ra i no - stri pet - ti; non ec -
riv - er Guard the shores, E - gyp - tians brave, Un - to
Da o - gni cor prorompa un grido: guerra e morte al - lo stra -
And un - to death the foe de - liv - er, E - gypt ne'er they shall en -
de' Nu - mi so - lo stan le sor - ti del guer -
in them con - fid - ing. Their pro - tection let us
cheg - gi che un sol gri - do: guer - ra, guer - ra e morte al - lo stra -
death the foe de - liv - er, E - gypt they nev - er, never shall en -
cheg - gi che un sol gri - do: guer - ra, guer - ra e morte al - lo stra -
death the foe de - liv - er, E - gypt they nev - er, never shall en -

Aida.
pp
(Per chi pian-go? per chi pian - go? per chi
(Whom to weep for? whom to pray for? whom to
Radamès.
grandioso
Sa - cro fre - mi - to di
Glo - ry's sa - cred thirst now
nier!
slave!
nier!
slave!
nier!
slave!
nier!
slave!
pp
pp
pre - go? qual po - ter m'av - vin - ce a lu - i! Deg - gio a -
pray for? Ah! what pow'r to him now binds me! Yet I
glo - ria tut - ta l'a - ni - ma m'in - ve - ste. Su! cor -
claims me, Now 'tis war a - lone in - flames me; On to

mar - lo - ed è co - stui
love, tho' all re - minds me
ria - mo al - la vit - to - ria! guer - ra,
vic - try! Naught we stay for! For - ward,
Amneris.
un ne - mi - co, u - no stra - nier!) Di mia man ri - ce - vi, o
That I love my coun - try's foe!) From my hand, thou warrior
guer - ra è mor - te al - lo stra - nier!
for - ward, and death to ev - 'ry foe!
pp
du - ce, il ves - sil - lo glo - ri - o - so; ti sia
glo - rious, Take thy stan - dard, aye vic - to - rious; Let it
pp
p
gui - da, ti si - a lu - ce del - la glo - ria sul sen -
ev - er lead thee on - ward To the foe - man's o - ver -

Aïda.
(Per chi
(Whom to
Amneris.
tier, ti sia
throw, yes, let it
Radamès.
Su! cor-
On! to
Messenger.
Su! cor -
On! to
The King.
Su! del Ni - lo al sa - cro
On! of Ni - lus' sa - cred
Ramphis.
Glo - ria ai Nu - mi, e o - gnun ram -
Glo - ry ren - der, glo - ry a -
Chorus of Priests.
Glo - ria,
Glo - ry
Glo - ria ai Nu - mi, e o - gnun ram -
Glo - ry ren - der, glo - ry a -
Chorus of Min. and Cap.
Su! del Ni - lo al sa - cro
On! of Ni - lus' sa - cred
Su! del Ni - lo al sa - cro
On! of Ni - lus' sa - cred
ff
stacc.

pian - go? per chi
weep for? whom to
gui - da, ti sia gui - da, ti sia
ev - er, let it ev - er lead thee
ria - mo, su! cor - ria - mo al - la vit -
vict' - ry, on! to vict' - ry! there's naught we
ria - mo, su! cor -
vict' - ry, on! to
li - do ac - cor - re - te E - gi - zii e -
riv - er Guard the shores, E - gyp - tians
men - ti ch'es - si reg - go - no gli e -
bid - ing To our Gods, the war - rior
glo - ria ai Nu - mi, chè in po -
glo - ry a - bid - ing To our Gods, the
men - ti ch'es - si reg - go - no gli e -
bid - ing To our Gods, the war - rior
li - do sien bar - rie - ra i no - stri
riv - er Guard the shores, E - gyp - tians
li - do sien bar - rie - ra i no - stri
riv - er Guard the shores, E - gyp - tians

pre - - go? per chi
pray for? whom to
lu - - ce, ti sia
on - - ward, e'er lead thee
to ria! Guer - - -
stay for! For - ward,
ria - mo al - la vit - to - ria! guer - ra e
vict' - ry, naught we stay for! For - - ward,
roi, da o - gni cor pro - rom - pa un
brave; Un - to death the foe de -
ven - ti, che in po - ter de' Nu - mi
guid - ing, In their pow'r a - lone con -
ter de' Nu - mi so - lo stan le
war - rior guid - ing, In their
ven - ti, che in po - ter de' Nu - mi
guid - ing, In their pow'r a - lone con -
pet - ti; non ec - cheg - gi che un sol
brave; Un - to death the foe de -
pet - ti; non ec - cheg - gi che un sol
brave; Un - to death the foe de -

pian - - - - go? per chi pre - -
pray for, whom to pray
lu - ce del - la glo - ria sul sen-
on - ward to the foe - man's o - ver
ra, guer - ra e mor - te al - lo stra-
ward, for - ward, and death, ay, death to ev' - ry
mor - te guer - ra e mor - te al - lo stra-
for - ward, for - ward, and death, ay, death to ev' - ry
gri - do: guer - ra, guer - ra e mor - te al - lo stra-
liv - er, For - ward, for - ward and death to ev' - ry
so - lo stan le sor - ti, le sor - ti, del guer-
pow - er still con - fid - ing, Pro - tec - tion let us
sor - ti, stan le sor - ti, le sor - ti del guer-
Gods all mor - tals guid - ing, their pro - tec - tion let us
so - lo stan le sor - ti, le sor - ti del guer-
fid - ing, Their pro - tec - tion, pro - tec - tion let us
gri - do: guer - ra, guer - ra e mor - te al - lo stra-
liv - er, For - ward, for - ward, and death to ev' - ry
gri - do: guer - ra, guer - ra e mor - te al - lo stra-
liv - er, For - ward, for - ward, and death to ev' - ry

Più mosso.
go?
for?
tier!
throw.
Guerra!
Battle!
nier!
foe!
Guerra!
Battle!
nier!
foe!
Guerra!
Battle!
nier! Guerra! guerra! guerra!
foe! Bat-tle! battle! bat-tle!
rier! Guerra! guerra! guerra!
crave! Bat-tle! battle! bat-tle!
rier! Guer-ra! guerra!
crave! Bat-tle! bat-tle!
rier! Guer-ra! guerra!
crave! Bat-tle! bat-tle!
nier! Guerra! guerra!
foe! Battle! bat-tle!
nier! Guerra! guerra!
foe! Battle! bat-tle!
Più mosso. (♩= 116)

incalz. sempre
(Deggio amar - lo, e veggo in
(Yet I love, tho' all re-
guerra! guerra! guer - ra! ster-mi -
bat-tle! bat-tle! bat - tle! No quar -
guer-ra!
bat - tle!
guerra!
bat-tle!
ff incalz. sempre

lui un ne - mi - co, u - no stra - nier! deg-gio a -
minds me That he is my coun-try's foe! Yet I
nio! guer - ra! guer - ra! ster - mi - nio! ster -
ter! bat - tle! bat - tle! No quar - ter! No
nio! guer - ra! guer - ra! ster - mi - nio! ster -
ter! bat - tle! bat - tle! No quar - ter! No
nio! guer - ra! guer - ra! ster - mi - nio! ster -
ter! bat - tle! bat - tle! No quar - ter! No
nio! guer - ra! guer - ra! ster - mi - nio! ster -
ter! bat - tle! bat - tle! No quar - ter! No
nio! guer - ra! guer - ra! ster - mi - nio! ster -
ter! bat - tle! bat - tle! No quar - ter! No
nio! ster - mi - nio al - l'in - va - sor! ster -
ter! bat - tle! bat - tle! No quar - ter! No
nio! ster - mi - nio al - l'in - va - sor! ster -
ter! bat - tle! bat - tle! No quar - ter! No
nio! ster - mi - nio al - l'in - va - sor! ster -
ter! bat - tle! bat - tle! No quar - ter! No
nio! ster - mi - nio al - l'in - va - sor! ster -
ter! bat - tle! bat - tle! No quar - ter! No

mar - - - - - lo, è un ne - mi - co, u - no stra -
love him, tho' he is my country's
mi - nio al - l'in - va - sor! ster - mi - nio al l'in - va -
quar - ter to an - y foe! No quar - ter to an - y
mi - nio al - l'in - va - sor! ster - mi - nio al l'in - va -
quar - ter to an - y foe! No quar - ter to an - y
mi - nio al - l'in - va - sor! ster - mi - nio al l'in - va -
quar - ter to an - y foe! No quar - ter to an - y
mi - nio al - l'in - va - sor! ster - mi - nio al l'in - va -
quar - ter to an - y foe! No quar - ter to an - y
mi - nio al - l'in - va - sor! ster - mi - nio al l'in - va -
quar - ter to an - y foe! No quar - ter to an - y
mi - nio al - l'in - va - sor! ster - mi - nio al - l'in - va -
quar - ter to an - y foe! No quar - ter to an - y
mi - nio al - l'in - va - sor! ster - mi - nio al - l'in - va -
quar - ter to an - y foe! No quar - ter to an - y
mi - nio al - l'in - va - sor! ster - mi - nio al - l'in - va -
quar - ter to an - y foe! No quar - ter to an - y
mi - nio al - l'in - va - sor! ster - mi - nio al - l'in - va -
quar - ter to an - y foe! No quar - ter to an - y

nier!)
foe!)
sor! guerra! guerra! guerra!
foe! battle! battle! battle!
sor! guerra! guerra! guerra!
foe! battle! battle! battle!
sor! guerra! guerra! guerra!
foe! battle! battle! battle!
sor! guer - ra! guer - ra! guer - ra! guer - ra!
foe! bat - tle! bat - tle! bat - tle! bat - tle!
sor! guer - ra! guer - ra! guer - ra! guer - ra!
foe! bat - tle! bat - tle! bat - tle! bat - tle!
sor! guer - ra! guer - ra! guer - ra! guer - ra!
foe! bat - tle! bat - tle! bat - tle! bat - tle!
sor! guer - ra! guer - ra! guer - ra! guer - ra!
foe! bat - tle! bat - tle! bat - tle! bat - tle!
sor! guerra! guerra! guerra!
foe! battle! battle! battle!
sor! guerra! guerra! guerra!
foe! battle! battle! battle!
ff

Ah! Ri-
Ah! May
(to Radamès) a piacere
guer - - ra! Ri-tor-na vin-ci-tor! Ri-
bat - - tle! May laurels crown thy brow! May
guer - - ra!
bat - - tle!
guer - - ra! Ri-
bat - - tle! May
guer - - ra! Ri-
bat - - tle! May
guer - - ra! Ri-
bat - - tle! May
guer - - ra! Ri-
bat - - tle! May
guer - - ra! Ri-
bat - - tle! May
guer - - ra! Ri-
bat - - tle! May
guer - - ra! Ri-
bat - - tle! May
col canto
ff a tempo

(exeunt all but Aïda.)
tor-na vin-ci-tor!
laurels crown thy brow!
tor-na vin-ci-tor!
laurels crown thy brow!
tor-na vin-ci-tor!
laurels crown thy brow!
tor-na vin-ci-tor!
laurels crown thy brow!
tor-na vin-ci-tor!
laurels crown thy brow!
tor-na vin-ci-tor!
lau-rels crown thy brow!
tor-na vin-ci-tor!
lau-rels crown thy brow!
tor-na vin-ci-tor!
lau-rels crown thy brow!
tor-na vin-ci-tor!
lau-rels crown thy brow!
col canto
a tempo
ff

Scene.

Aïda.

Allegro agitato. (𝅗𝅥 = 188)
Aïda.
Piano.
Ri-tor-na vin-ci - tor! E dal mio lab-bro u-
May lau-rels crown thy brow! What! can my lips pro-
ff
pp
scì l'em-pia pa - ro-la! Vin-ci - tor del pa-dre
nounce language so impious! Wish him vic-tor o'er my
f
mi - o_ di lui che im-pu-gna l'ar-mi per me_ per ri-do-nar-mi u-na
fa - ther_ o'er him who wag-es war but that I may be re-stor'd to my
pp
3
pa-tria, u-na reg-gia e il no-me il-lu-stre che qui ce-lar m'è for-za!
country, to my kingdom, to the high sta-tion I now perforce dis-sem-ble!
f

Vin-ci-tor de' miei fra-tel-li— on-d'io lo
Wish him con-qu'ror o'er my broth-ers— E'en now I
pp
veg-ga, tin-to del san-gue a-ma-to, tri-on-far nel
see him, stain'd with their blood so cher-ish'd, 'mid the clam'-rous
cresc.
f
plau-so dell' E-gi-zie co-or-ti!— E die-tro il
tri-umph of E-gyp-tian ba-tal-lions!— Be-hind his
f
car-ro, un Re— mio pa-dre— di ca-te-ne av-vin-to!—
cha-riot a King— my fa-ther— as a fet-ter'd cap-tive!—
ff

Più mosso. (𝅗𝅥 = 100.)
pp
L'in - sa - na pa - ro - la o Nu - mi sper - de - te! al
Ye Gods watch-ing o'er.... me, Those words deem un - spo - ken! A
se - no d'un pa - dre la fi - glia ren - de - te; strugge - - -
fa - ther re - store me, His daugh-ter heart-broken; Oh scat - - -
f
te, strugge - - - te, strug - ge - te le squa - dre dei
ter, oh scat - - - ter, oh scat - ter their ar - mies, for
f
no - stri op - pres - sor! Ah! sven - tu - ra - ta! che
ev - er crush our foe! Ah! what wild words do I
ff

Andante poco più lento della Iª volta.
dissi? e l'a-mor mi-o? Dun - que scordar pos-
utter? Of my af - fection Have I no re - col-
p cantabile
pp
s'i - - o que-sto fer - - vi - do a - mo-re che, oppres-sa e
lec - - tion? That sweet love that con - sol'd me, a cap-tive
schiava, co-me rag-gio di sol qui mi be - a - va? Im-pre-che-
pin-ing. Like some bright, sun - ny ray on my sad lot shin - ing? Shall I in-
pp
dolce
rò la morte a Ra-da - mès a lui ch'a-mo pur tan-to!
voke de-struction on the man for whom in love I languish!

Ah! non fu in ter - ra mai da più cru - de - - li an-
Ah! nev - er yet on earth liv'd one whose heart was
go-scie un co - re af - franto!
torn by wild - er anguish!
Allegro giusto poco agitato (♩=100)
triste e dolce
I sa - cri no - mi di pa - dre - d'a-
Those names so ho - ly, of fa - ther, of
rall.
morendo
con espress.
ppp
man - te, nè prof - fe - rir pos - s'i - o, nè ri - - cor-
lov - er, No more dare I now ut - ter or e'en re-
m. s.
dar Per l'un per l'al - tro con - fu - sa tre-
call; A - bash'd and trembling, to heav'n fain would
pp

man- te_ io pian- ge- re vor- rei_ vor - rei pre-
hov- er My pray'rs for both, for both my tears would
m. s.
con più forza
gar. Ma la mia pre - ce in bestem - mia si
fall. Ah! all my prayers seem transform'd to blas-
pp
mu- ta_ de- lit- to è il pian- to a me_ col - pa il so-
pheming, To suf- fer is a crime, dark sin to
spir_ in not - te cu - pa la men - te è per-
sigh; Thro' dark - est night I do wan - der as
p
du- ta_ e nell' an - sia cru- del vor- rei ___ mo- rir.
dreaming And so cru - el my woe, I fain ___ would die.
13573

Cantabile.
con espress.
Nu - mi, pie - tà del mio sof - frir! Spe - me non v'ha
Mer - ci - ful gods! look from on high! Pit - y these tears
pp
pp
pel mio do - lor_ A - mor fa -
hope - less - ly shed_ Love, fa - tal
tal tre - men - do a - mor spez - za - mi il
pow'r, mys - tic_ and dread, Break thou_ my
p
cor,_ fam - mi mo - rir! Nu - mi,_ pie -
heart,_ now let me die! Mer - ci - ful
p

poco string.
tà del mio sof - frir, ah! pie - tà, Nu - mi, pie -
gods! look from on high, ah! Oh hear, mer - ci - ful
f
tà del mio sof - frir, Nu - mi, pie - tà del mio sof -
gods! oh hear my cry! mer - ci - ful gods! oh hear my
f
pp
perdendosi.
(exit.)
frir, pie - tà, pie - tà del mio sof - frir!
cry, oh hear, oh hear, ye gods on high.
ppp
morendo.
ppp
ppp
dolce.
dim.
morendo.

Grand Scene of the Consecration, and first Finale.

SCENE II. Interior of the Temple of Vulcan at Memphis.

A mysterious light from above. A long row of columns, one behind the other, vanishing in darkness. Statues of various deities. In the middle of the stage, above a platform covered with carpet, rises the altar, surmounted with sacred emblems. Golden tripods emitting the fumes of incense.

un po' stent.
chia - - mo!
voke thee!
morendo
chia - - mo!
voke thee!
Ramphis.
pp
Tu che dal nul-la hai trat-to
Thou who mad'st ev-'ry crea-ture,
pp
Chorus of Priests.
Tu che dal nul-la hai trat-to
Thou who mad'st ev-'ry crea-ture,
pp
Tu che dal nul-la hai trat-to
Thou who mad'st ev-'ry crea-ture,
pp morendo col canto
stent.
l'on - de, la ter-ra, il ciel, noi t'in-vo - chia - mo!
Earth, wa-ter, air and fire, Lo, we in - voke thee!
stent.
l'on - de, la ter-ra, il ciel, noi t'in-vo - chia - mo!
Earth, wa-ter, air and fire, Lo, we in - voke thee!
stent.
l'on - de, la ter-ra, il ciel, noi t'in-vo - chia - mo!
Earth, wa-ter, air and fire, Lo, we in - voke thee!
f

High Priestess.
Priestesses.
Im - men - so, immen - so Fthà, del mon - do
Al - mighty, al-mighty Phthà, that mak - est
spir - to fe - con - da - tor, ah! ah!
all fruit-ful things grow rife, Hail! Hail!
noi t'in - vo - chia - mo!
lo, we in - voke thee!
Noi t'in - vo - chia - mo!
Lo, we in - voke thee!
ff
f
p
pp
stent.
morendo col canto
Ramphis.
Nu - me che del tuo spi - ri - to sei figlio e ge - ni - tor, noi t'in - vo - chia -
Thou, who of thine own na - ture art son as well as sire, lo, we in - voke
Priests.

High Priestess.
Priestesses.
Fuo - co in-cre-a - to, e-ter - no,
Flame un-cre-at - ed, e-ter - nal,
mo!
thee!
Priests.
mo!
thee!
ff
on - de eb - be lu - ce il sol, ah!
Fount of all light a - bove, hail!
f
ah! noi t'in-vo-chia - mo!
hail! lo, we in-voke thee!
pp
morendo
Noi t'in-vo-chia - mo!
Lo, we in-voke thee!
pp
morendo
col canto

Ramphis.
pp
stent.
Vi - ta del-l'U-ni - ver - so, mi - to d'e-ter-no a - mor, noi t'in-vo -
Life - giv-er u - ni - ver - sal, Source of un-end-ing love, Thee we in -
Priests.
pp
stent.
Vi - ta del-l'U-ni - ver - so, mi - to d'e-ter-no a - mor, noi t'in-vo -
Life - giv-er u - ni - ver - sal, Source of un-end-ing love, Thee we in -
pp
stent.
Vi - ta del-l'U-ni - ver - so, mi - to d'e-ter-no a - mor, noi t'in-vo -
Life - giv-er u - ni - ver - sal, Source of un-end-ing love, Thee we in -
ppp
p
Im - men - so Fthà!
Al - might - y Phthà!
ppp
p
Im - men - so Fthà!
Al - might - y Phthà!
fp
chiam! noi t'in-vo-chiam!
voke! thee we in - voke!
fp
chiam! noi t'in-vo-chiam!
voke! thee we in - voke!
fp
chiam! noi t'in-vo-chiam!
voke! thee we in - voke!
pp

Sacred Dance of Priestesses.

Allegretto. (♩= 96.)

p dolciss.
tr
m. s.
(Radamès enters unarmed, and goes up to the altar)
f
m.s.

(A silver veil is placed on the head of Radamès.)

Priestesses.
Im - - men - so
Al - - might - y
Priests.
Fthà!
Phthà!
(to Radamès)
Ramphis.
Noi t'in - vo - chiam!
Thee we in - voke!
Mor - tal, di - let - to ai
Of Gods the fa - vor'd
Recit.
Nu - mi, a te fi - da - te son d'E - git - to le sor - ti.
mor - tal, to thee con - fid - ed be the wel - fare of E - gypt.

Il sa - cro bran - do dal Dio tem - pra - to, per tua man di -
Thy wea - pon, tem - per'd by hand im - mor - tal, in thy hand shall
pp
ven - ti ai ne - mi - ci ter - ror, fol - go - re, mor - te.
bring to the foe - men a - larm, a - go - ny, ter - ror!
Priests.
Tutti.
f
Il sa - cro
This wea - pon,
f
Il sa - cro
This wea - pon,
f
bran - do dal Dio tem - pra - to, per tua man di - ven - ti ai ne - mi - ci ter -
tem - per'd by hand im - mor - tal, in thy hand shall bring to the foe - men a -
bran - do dal Dio tem - pra - to, per tua man di - ven - ti ai ne - mi - ci ter -
tem - per'd by hand im - mor - tal, in thy hand shall bring to the foe - men a -

Ramphis.
fol - go - re, mor - - te.
a - go - ny, ter - - ror.
ror, fol - go - re, mor - - te.
larm, a - go - ny, ter - - ror.
ror, fol - go - re, mor - - te.
larm, a - go - ny, ter - - ror.
ff
pp
Larga la frase.
(Turning to the god)
cantabile
Nu - me, cu - sto - de e vin - di - ce
Grave. (♩= 66.)
Hear us, oh guardian de - i - ty,
pp
ten.
di questa sa - cra ter - ra, la ma - no tua di - sten - - di
Our sacred land pro - tect - ing, Thy mighty hand ex - tend - - ing,
ten.
Radamès.
so - vra, so - vra l'e - gi - zio suol. Nu - me, che Du - ce ed
dan - ger, danger from E - gypt ward. Hear us, each mortal
pp dolciss.
poco cresc.
ppp stacc.

Radamès.
ar - bi-tro sei d'o-gni u-ma - na guer - ra,
des - ti-ny war's dread-ful course di-rect - ing,
Ramphis.
La ma-no tu-a, la ma-no tuo di-
Thy mighty hand, thy might-y hand ex-
pro - teg-gi tu, di-fen - - di d'E-git-to il sa-cro, il sa-cro
Aid un-to E-gypt send - - ing, Keep o'er her children, her children
sten-di so-vra l'e-gi-zio, l'e-gi - zio
tend-ing, dan-ger from E-gypt, from E - gypt
suol.
ward.
suol.
ward.
2d TENORS.
Nu - - me, cu-sto-de e
Hear us, oh guardian
Priests.
2d BASSES.
Nu - - me, cu-sto-de e vin-di-ce di
Hear us, oh guar-dian de-i-ty, our

Nu - - - me, cu - sto - de e vin - di - ce di que - sta sa - cra
Hear us, oh guardian de - i - ty, our sa - cred land pro -
1st TENORS.
vin - di - ce di que - sta sa - - cra
de - i - ty, our sa - cred land pro - - -
Nu - - me, cu - sto - de e
Hear us, oh guar - dian
1st BASSES.
que - - - sta sa - - cra
sa - - - cred land pro - - -
Radamès.
Ramphis.
ff
Nu - - me, cu - sto - de ed
Hear us, oh guar - dian
ter - ra,
tect - ing,
ter - ra,
tect - ing,
la ma - - no
Thy might - y
vin - di - ce,
de - i - ty,
unis.
ter - ra,
tect - ing,
Nu - - me, cu - sto - de e
Hear us, oh guar - dian

Pro - - - - teg - gi tu,
Aid un - to us,
ar- - bi - tro di que - sta sa - cra
de- - - i - ty, our sa - cred land pro-
tu- - - a, la ma - no tua di-
hand, thy might - y hand ex-
vin- - di - ce di que - sta sa - cra
de- - - i - ty, our sa - cred land pro-
8
pro - teg- - gi tu, di - fen - di
Aid un- - to E - gypt send - ing,
ter- - ra, la ma - no tua di -
tect- - - ing, thy might - y hand ex -
sten- - di so - - vra le -
tend- - - ing, dan - - ger from
ter- - ra, la ma - no tua di
tect- - - ing, thy might - y hand ex -
8

d'E - git - to il sa - cro, il sa - cro
Keep o'er her chil - dren, her chil - dren
sten- - -di so - vra, so - vra l'e - gi - zio
tend- - -ing, dan - ger, dan-ger from E - gypt
so - vra l'e - gi - zio
dan - ger from E - gypt
gi- - -zio, so - vra l'e- - -gi - zio
E- - -gypt, dan - ger from E - gypt
sten- - -di so - vra, so - vra l'e - gi - zio
tend- - -ing, dan - ger, dan-ger from E - gypt
ff
Più mosso, come prima.
High-Priestess with 1st Sopranos. (Interior)
Pos- - -sen - te, pos - sen - te Fthà,
Al- - -might - y, al - might - y Phtha,
f
suol! Pos- - -sen - te
ward! Al- - -might - y
f
suol! Pos- - -sen - te
ward! Al- - -might - y
f
suol! Pos- - -sen - te
ward! Al- - -might - y
f
suol! Pos- - -sen - te
ward! Al- - -might - y
Più mosso, come prima.
f
ff

f
del mon - do cre - a - tor,
who wak - est life in all,
Fthà, spir- -to fe - con - da -
Phthà, who mak - est all things
Fthà, spir- -to fe - con - da -
Phthà, who mak - est all things
Fthà, spir- -to fe - con - da -
Phthà, who mak - est all things
Fthà, spir- -to fe - con - da -
Phthà, who mak - est all things
f
ff
ah! ah!
Hail! Hail!
tor, tu che dal nul - la hai tratto il mon - do, noi t'in-vochia - mo!
rife, hail, thou who mad - est all things cre-at - ed, lo, we invoke thee!
tor, tu che dal nulla hai tratto il mondo,
rife, hail, thou who madest all things cre - ated,
tor,
rife,
tor, tu che dal
rife, hail, thou who
mf

Ramphis.
tu che dal nul- -la hai trat - to l'on- -de,
hail, thou whomad- -est all things cre-at - ed,
tu che dal nul- -la hai trat - to l'on - de,
hail, thou who mad- -est all things cre-at- -ed,
nul - -la hai trat - to l'on- -de, la ter-ra,il
mad - est all things cre - at- -ed, earth, wa-ter,
Pos - sen - te Fthà!
Al - might - y Phthà!
Radamès.
Noi t'in - vo - chia-
lo! we in - voke
Ramphis.
la ter - ra,il cie- -lo, noi t'in - vo - chia-
earth, wa - ter, heav- -en, lo! we in - voke
la ter - ra,il cie- -lo, noi t'in - vo - chia-
earth, wa - ter, heav- -en, lo! we in - voke
cie - lo, noi t'in - vo - chiam, noi t'in - vo - chia-
heav - en, thee we in - voke, lo! we in - voke
ff

ppp
mo! tu che dal nul-la hai trat-to il mon-do, noi t'in-vo-
thee! Hail, thou who mad'st all things cre-at-ed, lo, we in-
dim
p
Spi-ri-to a-ni-ma-
Thou that mak-est all things
chia- -mo!
voke thee!
morendo

tor, spir - - - - to fe - con - da -
rife, thou that mak't all things
pppp
noi t'in - vo - chiam!
thee we in - voke!
pppp
noi t'in - vo - chiam!
thee we in - voke!
pppp
noi t'in - vo - chiam!
thee we in - voke!
pppp
noi t'in - vo - chiam!
thee we in - voke!
ppp
3
tor, im - - - men - - so
rife, Al - - - might - - y
noi t'in - vo - chiam!
thee we in - voke!
noi t'in - vo - chiam!
thee we in - voke!
noi t'in - vo - chiam!
thee we in - voke!
noi t'in - vo - chiam!
thee we in - voke!

Fthà.
Phthà.
(pausa lunga.)
immenso
almighty
pp
noi t'invochiam!
thee we invoke!
immenso Fthà! immenso
almighty Phthà! almighty
ff
noi t'invochiam
thee we invoke.
ppp
Fthà!
Phthà!

End of Act I.

Act II.

Introduction.

Scene, Chorus of Women and Dance of Moorish Slaves.

SCENE I. A hall in the apartments of Amneris.

Amneris surrounded by female slaves who attire her for the triumphal feast. Tripods emitting perfumed vapors. Young Moorish slaves waving feather-fans.

— fra gl'inni ei plau - si
— his glo - ry prais - ing,
er - ge al la glo - ria il vol,
Heavenward waft a name,
plau - si
prais - ing,
er - ge al - la glo - ria il vol,
Heav - en - ward waft a — name,
al
Whose
al par
Whose deeds,
d'un Dio ter - ri - bi - le,
the sun out - blaz - ing,
del sol?
Outshine
par d'un Dio — ter - ri - bi - le,
deeds, the sun — out - blaz - ing,
ful - gen - te al par del sol?
Out - shine his dazzling flame,
ful - gen - te al par del sol?
Out - shine his dazzling flame!
Vie - ni: sul crin ti
Come, bind thy flow - ing
ful - gen - te al par del sol?
Outshine his dazzling flame!
pp
f
ppp
ff
dolciss.

pio - va - no
tress - es round
con - te - - sti ai
With lau - - rel,
Vie - ni: sul crin ti pio - va - no
Come, bind thy flow - ing tress - es round
pp
lau - - ri, ai lau - - - ri i fior; suo - nin di glo - ria i
lau - - rel, and per - - - fum'd flow'rs, While loud our songs of
con - te - sti ai lau - - - ri i fior;
With lau - rel and with flow'rs.
can - ti - ci coi can - ti - ci d'a -
praise resound To cel - e - brate love's
suo - nin di glo - ria i can - ti - ci coi
While loud our songs of praise resound To
pp

Amneris.
con espansione
(Ah! vie - - - ni, vie-ni a-mor mio, m'i-
(Ah! come, love, come love, with rap-ture
ppp grazioso
mor, coi can - ti - ci d'a - mor.
pow'r, to cel - e - brate love's pow'rs.
ppp
can - ti - ci d'a - mor.
cel - - e - brate love's pow'rs.
dolciss.
pp
neb-bria, fammi be - a - to il cor, fammi be - a - to il cor.)
fill me, to joy my heart re - store, to joy my heart re - store.)
morendo
Or
Ah!
Or do - - ve son le bar-ba-re
Ah! where are now the foes who dar'd
do - ve son le bar-ba-re or - de, del - lo stra
where are now the foes who dar'd E - gypt's brave sons at-

or - de del - lo stra-nier? Sie-co -
E-gypt's brave sons at - tack? As doves
nier? Sie - co - me neb - bia
tack? As doves are by the
- me neb - bia spar - ve - ro al sof - fio,
are by the ea - gle scar'd, Our war-rior,
spar - ve - ro al sof - fio del guer - rier,
ea - gle scar'd, Our war - riors drove them back,
al sof - fio del guer - rier. Vie - ni: glo-ria il
our war - riors drove them back. Now, wreaths of tri-umph
al sof - fio del guer - rier.
our war - riors drove them back.
dolciss.

pre - mio
glo - rious
rac - co - gli o vin - ci -
The vic - tor's brow shall
Vie - ni: di glo - ria il pre - mio
Now wreaths of tri - umph glo - rious
tor, rac - co - gli o vin - ci - tor; t'ar - ri - se la vit -
crown, The vic - tor's brow shall crown, And love, o'er him vic -
rac - co - gli o vin - ci - tor;
The vic - tor's brow shall crown,
to - ria,
to - rious,
t'ar - ri - de - rà l'a -
Shall smooth his war - like
t'ar - ri - se la vit - to - ria, t'ar-
And love, o'er him vic - to - rious, Shall
pp

Amneris.
con espansione.
(Ah! vie - ni, vie - ni, a-mor mio, rav -
(Ah! come love, come love, let thy voice
pp grazioso.
mor, t'ar - ri - de - rà l'a - mor.
frown, shall smooth his war-like frown.
ri - de - rà l'a - mor.
smooth his war-like frown.
dolce.
pp
dim.
morendo.
vi - va-mi d'un caro ac-cento an - cor, d'un caro ac - cento an - cor!)
thrill me with ac-cents dear once more, with ac-cents dear once more!)
Più mosso. (♩ = 152)
Dance of young Moorish Slaves.
The female slaves continue
attiring Amneris.
leggerissimo
ppp

pp
pp
mf
leggiero
pp
marcato

ff
f
stacc.
ff
Chorus.
Soprano I.
Vie - ni: sul crin ti
Come,bindthy flowing
Tempo I.
p

pio - va - no
tress - es round
con - te - sti ai
With lau - rel,
2d SOP. & CONTR.
Vie - ni: sul crin ti pio - va - no
Come, bind thy flow - ing tress - es round
lau - ri, ai lau - ri i fior;
lau - rel and per - fum'd flow'rs,
suo - nin di glo - ria i
While loud our songs of
con - te - sti ai lau - ri i fior;
With lau - rel and with flow'rs,
can - ti - ci
praise re-sound
coi can - ti - ci d'a -
To cel - e - brate love's
suo - nin di glo - ria i can - ti - ci
While loud our songs of praise re-sound
coi
To
pp

Amneris.
con espansione
(Ah! vie -
(Ah! come,
pp e stacc.
ppp
mor, coi can - ti - ci d'a - mor,
pow'rs, to cel - e - brate love's pow'rs,
can - ti - ci d'a - mor, coi
cel - e - brate love's pow'rs, to
pp
ni, vie - ni, a - mor mio, m'i - neb - bria, fam - mi be - a - to il
love, come love, with rap - ture fill me, to joy my heart re -
d'a - mor,
love's pow'rs,
can - ti -
cel - e -
Tempo I.
cor, fam-mi be - a - to il cor!) Si -
store, to joy my heart re - store!) Be
d'a - mor.
love's pow'rs.
ci d'a - mor.
brate love's pow'rs.
Tempo I. (♩= 72.)
m. d. cantabile

len-zio! A-i-da ver-so noi s'a-van-za... Fi-glia de'
si-lent! A-i-da hith-er now ad-vanc-es... Child of the
(at a sign from Amneris the slaves retire)
(enter Aïda)
vin-ti, il suo do-lor m'è sa-cro.
con-quer'd, to me her grief is sa-cred.
Nel ri-ve-der-la, il dub-bio a-tro-ce in... me si de-sta...
On her ap-pearance, my soul a-gain with...doubt is tor-tur'd.
Allegro risoluto.
Il mi-ste-ro fa-tal, si squar-ci al fi-ne!
It shall now be re-veal'd, the fa-tal mys-t'ry!
col canto
pp

Scene and Duet.

Aïda and Amneris.

Più mosso. (♩=100)
li - - ce es - ser pos - s'i - - o, lun - gi dal suol na -
how can I be hap - - py, far from my na - tive
f
ti - o - qui do - ve i - gno - ta m'è la sor - te del pa - dre e dei fra -
coun - try, where I can nev - er know what fate may be - fall my fa - ther,
Come prima. (♩=88)
Amneris.
tel - li? Ben ti com - pian - go! pu - re han - no un con - fi - ne i
broth - ers? Deep - ly you move me! yet no hu - man sor - row is
ff
ppp
ma - li di quag - giù... Sa - ne - rà il tem - po le an -
last - ing here be - low... Time will bring com - fort and
pp
pp

go-scie del tuo co - re... e più che il tem - po, un Dio pos-
heal your pres-ent an - guish... great - er than time e'en the heal-ing
Allegro animato.
(much moved.)
sotto voce a parte.
Aïda.
(A - mo - re, a - mo - re! gau - dio... tor -
(Oh love, sweet pow - er! oh joy tor -
pp
sen - te... a - mo - - re.
pow - er of love... is.
Allegro animato. (♩= 112)
pp
pp dolce.
men - to... so - a - ve eb - brez - za, an - sia cru - del... ne' tuoi do -
ment - ing... Rap - tu - rous mad - ness, bliss fraught with woes... Thy pangs most
lo - ri la vi - ta io sen - to... un tuo... sor -
cru - el a life con - tent - ing... Thy smiles... en -
Amneris. sotto voce.
(Ah! quel pal - lo - re... quel tur - ba - men - to
(Yon dead - ly pal - lor... her bo - som pant - ing,

a poco a poco cresc.
ri - so mi schiu-de il ciel, un tuo sor-
chant - ing bright heav'n dis-close, Thy smiles en-
sve-lan l'ar-ca - - - na feb-bre d'a-mor.
Tell of love's pas - - - sion, tell of love's woes.
pp leggeriss.
ri - - so mi schiu-de il ciel, ne' tuoi do-
chant - - ing bright heav'n dis-close, Thy pangs most
D'in-ter-ro-gar-la quasi ho sgo-men-to
Her heart to ques-tion, cour-age is wanting
f
ff e string. poco a
lo-ri la vi-ta jo sen-to un tuo sor-ri-so mi schiu-de il
cru-el a life con-tent-ing Thy smiles en-chant-ing bright heav'n dis-
di-vi-do l'an-sie del su - o ter-
My bo-som feels of her tor - - ture the
poco

Poco più lento.
ciel!)
close!)
(eyeing her fixedly)
ror.)
throes.)
Eb - ben: qual nuo - vo
Now say, what new e -
Poco più lento. (♩ = 88)
espressivo
p
fer - mi - to t'as - sal, gen - til A - i - da?
mo - tion so doth sway my fair A - i - da?
I tuoi se - gre - ti
Thy se - cret thought re -
dolce
sve - la - mi, al - l'a - mor mi - o, al - l'a - mor mio t'af - fi - da. Tra i for - ti che pu -
veal to me: come, trust se - cure - ly, come, trust in my af - fec - tion. A - mong the warriors
dolce
gna - ro - no del - la tua pa - tria a dan - no qual - cu - no un dol - ce af -
brave who fought fa - tal - ly 'gainst thy coun - try it may be that one has
p
dolciss.
p

Aïda.
Che par - li?
What mean'st thou?
fan-no_ for-se_ a te in cor de - stò? _ A tut-ti_
wak-end in thee gentle thoughts of love? _ The cru-el_
bar- ba- ra non si mo - strò la sor - te_ Se in cam-po il du - ce im-
fate of war not all a - like em - brac - es_ And then the daunt-less
Più mosso.
Che mai di - ce - sti! mi - se - ra! _
What dost thou tell me! wretch - ed fate! _
pa-vido cad-de tra-fit-to a mor-te. _
war-rior who leads the host may per-ish. _
Più mosso. (♩ = 112)
cresc.
f

Mi - - se-ra!
Wretch - - ed fate!
Sì Ra-da-mès da' tuoi fu spento E pianger
Yes Ra-da-mès by thine is slaughter'd and canst thou
pp
mf
p
Per sem - pre io pian - - ge -
For ev - er my tears shall
puo - i?
mourn him?
Gli
The
rò!
flow!
Av-ver - si sem-pre a me fu - ro i
Ce-les - tial fa - vor to me was ne'er ex-
Dei t'han ven - di - ca - ta
gods have wrought thee vengeance
ff

Nu-mi_
tend-ed_
ff (breaking out with violence)
Tre - - ma! in cor ti les-si_ tu
Trem - - ble! thou art dis-cov-er'd_ thou
ff
pp
p
I - o!_
I love!_
l'a - mi_ Non men - ti - re!_ Un det-to an-
lov'st him_ Ne'er de - ny it!_ Nay, to con-
f
co - ra e il ve - ro sa - prò_
found thee I need but a word_
f a piacere
Fis - sa - mi in
Gaze on my
ff
p
vol - to_ io t'in - gan - na - va_ Ra-da-mès
vis - age_ I told thee false - ly_ Ra-da-mès_
ppp col canto

Aïda (kneeling with rapture)
Vi - - - - - ve! ah gra - zie, o
Liv - - - - - eth! Gods, I
vi - ve
liv - eth
ff tutta forza
Nu - mi!
thank ye!
a piacere
E an-cor mentir tu spe-ri? Si tu
Dost hope still now de-ceive me? Yes thou
f
ppp
pp
l'a - mi Ma l'a-mo an-ch'io in-ten-di
lov'st him But so do I dost hear my
col canto
tu? son tua ri - va-le fi - glia de' Fa-ra-
words? be - hold thy ri-val, here in a Pharaoh's

Aïda. (Drawing herself up with pride.)
o - ni_ Mia ri - va - le! eb - ben sia pu - re_ An -
daughter_ Thou my ri - val! what tho' it were so_ For
pp cresc. e string.
(checking herself and falling at the feet of Amneris.)
ch'io_ son tal_ Ah!
I, I too_ Ah!
f
ff
che dis - si mai? pie - tà! per - do - no!
heed not my words! oh, spare! for give me!
p
Adagio. (♩ = 60.)
Cantabile espress.
ah! pie - tà ti pren - da del mio do -
ah! on all my an - guish sweet pit - y
p

lor— È ve - ro, io l'a - mo d'immen - so a -
take— 'Tis true, for his love I all else for -
mor— Tu sei fe - li - ce— tu sei pos -
sake— While thou art might - y, all joys thy
sen - te - io— vi - vo so - lo— per que - sto a -
dow - er, Naught save my love now— is left for
Amneris.
mor! Tre - ma, vil schia - va! spez - za il tuo co - re - se - gnar tua
me! Tremble, vile bond - maid! Dy - ing heart - broken, Soon shall thou

mor - te può_ que-st'a - mo - re_Del tuo de-sti-no ar-bi-tra
rue_ the love_ thou hast spo-ken. Do I not hold thee fast in my
Aïda.
Tu sei fe -
While thou art
so_no, d'o-dio e vendet-ta le fu-rie ho in cor.
power, Hatred and vengeance my heart owes for thee!
li - ce_ tu sei pos - sen - te_io_ vi - vo
hap - py_ all joys thy dow - er, Naught save my
Tre - ma, vil schia - va!
Trem - ble, vile me - nial!

poco incalzando
so - - lo __ per que - - st'a - mor! pie - tà! pie-
love now _ is left to me! On all, on
spez-za il tuo cor, spez-za il tuo
Thy brok - en heart shall rue the
pp poco incalzando
tà! ti pren - - da del mio do - lor __ pie-tà! pie-
all my an - - guish, sweet pit - y take __ Oh spare! oh
cor, tre-ma, vil schia - - va! del tuo de-sti - no arbi-tra jo
love that thou hast spok - - en! Do I not hold thee in my
tà! ti pren - - - - - - da del mi - o __ do-
spare! take pit - - - - - y, take pit - y __ on
son, d'o-dio e ven-det - ta le fu - rie ho in cor, le fu - rie in
pow'r, Ha-tred and ven - geance my heart owes for thee, ay, owes for

Aïda.
Allegro marziale.
lor.
me!
Amneris.
cor.
thee!
Soprano I & II.
ff
Su! del
On! of
Tenor.
ff
Su! del
On! of
Bass.
ff
Allegro marziale. (♩=100)
ff
ff
Amneris.
ff
Al - la pom - pa che s'ap-pre - sta, me-co o schia - va, as - si - ste-
In the pa - geant now pre-par - ing Shall a part by thee be
Ni - lo al sa - cro li - do sien bar - rie - ra i no - stri
Ni - lus' sa - cred riv - er Guard the shores, E - gyp - tians
Ni - lo al sa - cro li - do sien bar - rie - ra i no - stri
Ni - lus' sa - cred riv - er Guard the shores, E - gyp - tians
ff

ra - i; tu pro - stra - ta nel - la
tak - en; While be - fore me thou in
pet - ti; non ec - cheg - gi che un sol
brave, Un - to death the foe de -
pet - ti; non ec - cheg - gi che un sol
brave, Un - to death the foe de -
pol - ve - re, io sul tro - no ac - can - to al
dust art prone, I shall share the roy - al
gri - do: guer - ra, guer - ra e mor - te al - lo stra -
liv - er, E - gypt they nev - er, they nev - er shall en -
gri - do: guer - ra, guer - ra e mor - te al - lo stra -
liv - er, E - gypt they nev - er, they nev - er shall en -

Poco più vivo.
Aïda.
Ah! pie - tà! che più mi re - sta? un de - ser - to è la mia
Pray thee, spare a heart de - spair - ing! Life's to me a void for -
Re.
throne!
nier!
slave!
nier!
slave!
Poco più vivo. (♩=100.)
pp
vi - ta; vi - vi e re - gna, il tuo fu - ro - re io tra bre - ve pla - che -
sak - en; Live and reign, thy an - ger blight - ing, I shall soon no lon - ger
rò. Que - st'a - mo - re che t'ir - ri - ta nel - la tom - ba spe - gne -
brave, Soon this love, thy hate in - vit - ing, Shall be bur - ied in the
rò.
grave. Amneris.
Vien, mi se - gui, ap - pren - de -
Come, now fol - low, I will
f
p

Ah! pie - tà!
Ah! then spare!
ra - i se lot- -tar tu puoi con
show thee wheth - er thou canst vie with
que - st'a-
soon this
me, se lot-tar tu puoi, tu puoi con me,
me, wheth-er thou canst vie, canst vie with me,
pp
f
ff
mor nel la tom-
love shall be bur-
ap-pren-de-rai se lot-tar tu puoi
yes, I will show thee if thou canst vie,
ff
pp

- ba io spe - gne - rò, pie -
- ied with - in the grave, ah
tu puoi con me, vie -
canst vie with me, Come
Guer - ra e mor -
Doom'd to death the
Guer - ra e mor -
Doom'd to death the
tà! pie - tà!
spare! ah spare!
ni, mi se - - gui,
now, and fol - - low!
te, guer - ra e mor - te al - lo stra - nier!
foe, E - gypt ne'er shall they en - slave!
te, guer - ra e mor - te al - lo stra - nier!
foe, E - gypt ne'er shall they en - slave!
ff

Amneris.
e ap - pren - de - ra - i se lot - tar tu puoi con
for I will show thee wheth - er thou canst vie with
Aÿda.
Nu - mi, pie -
Pow - ers a -
me.
me!
guer - ra e mor - te al - lo stra - nier!
E - gypt ne'er shall they en - slave!
guer - ra e mor - te al - lo stra - nier!
E - gypt ne'er shall they en - slave!
ppp

tà del mio mar - tir, spe - me non
bove, pit - y my woe, Hope have I
v'ha, spe - me non v'ha pel mi - o do - lor; Nu - mi, pie -
none, hope have I none now here be - low; Deign, ye Im -
tà del mi - o sof - frir, Nu - mi, pie - tà! pie -
mor - tals, mer - cy to show; Ye gods, ah spare! ah
tà! pie - tà!
spare! ah spare!
ppp
f
morendo.

Grand Finale II.

SCENE II. An avenue to the City of Thebes.

In front, a clump of Palms. Right hand, a temple dedicated to Ammon. Left hand, a throne with a purple canopy: At back, triumphal arch. The stage is crowded with people.

Enter the King followed by Officials, Priests, Captains, Fan-bearers, Standard-bearers. Afterwards Amneris, with Aïda and slaves. The King takes his seat on the throne. Amneris places herself at his left hand.

SOPRANO I.
a tempo come prima.
Chorus of People.
Gloria all' E-git-to, ad I - si - de che il sa-cro suol pro - teg - ge! Al
Glo - ry to I - sis, who from all Ward-eth a-way dis - as - ter! To
SOPRANO II.
TENOR.
BASS.
ff a tempo come prima.
Re che il Del-ta reg - ge, al Re che il Del - ta reg-
E-gypt's roy - al mas - ter, to E - gypt's roy - al mas-
reg - ge
mas - ter

pesante e stent.
ge in - ni fe - sto-si al - ziam!
ter Raise we our fest - al song!
Glo - ria!
Glo - ry!
pesante e stent.
in - ni fe - sto-si al - ziam!
Raise we our fest - al song!
pesanti.
mf
Glo - ria!
Glo - ry!

Glo - ria al Re! Glo - - ria, glo - -
Glo - ry, oh King! Glo - - ry, glo - -
Glo - ria, glo - ria,
Glo - ry, glo - ry,
Glo - ria al Re! Glo - ria, glo - ria,
Glo - ry, oh King! Glo - ry, glo - ry,
Glo - ria, glo - ria,
Glo - ry, glo - ry,
cresc. e stringendo a poco
ria, glo - - ria! In - ni al - ziam, in - ni al - ziam! Glo -
ry, glo - - ry! Raise we our song, raise we our song! Glo -
glo - ria! In - ni al - ziam, in - ni al - ziam! Glo -
glo - ry! Raise we our song, raise we our song! Glo -
glo - ria! In - ni al - ziam, in - ni al - ziam! Glo -
glo - ry! Raise we our song, raise we our song! Glo -
glo - ria! In - ni al - ziam, in - ni al - ziam! Glo -
glo - ry! Raise we our song, raise we our song! Glo -
a poco

ria al Re! In-ni fe-sto-si, fe-sto-si al-
ry, oh King! Our fes-tal song, raise we our fes-tal
ria al Re! In-ni fe-sto-si al-
ry, oh King! Raise we our song, our fes-tal
ria al Re, al Re! In-ni fe-sto-si al-
ry, oh King, oh King! Raise we our song, our fes-tal
ria al Re, al Re! In-ni fe-sto-si al-
ry, oh King, oh King! Raise we our song, our fes-tal
tornando come prima
cantabile
ziam! SOPRANI SOLI. S'in-trec-ci il lo-to al lau-ro sul
song! The lau-rel with the lo-tus bound the
ziam! S'in-trec-ci il lo-to al lau-ro sul
song! The lau-rel with the lo-tus bound the
ziam!
song!
ziam!
song!
tornando al I. tempo

crin dei vin - ci - to - ri! nem - bo gen - til di fio - ri
vic - tors' brows en - wreath - ing! Let flow'rs sweet per - fume breath - ing,
vin - ci - to - ri!
brows en - wreath - ing!
crin dei vin - ci - to - ri! nem - bo gen - til di fio - ri -
vic - tors' brows en - wreath - ing! Let flow'rs sweet per - fume breath - ing,
sten - da sull' ar - mi un vel! Dan - ziam, fanciulle e - gi - zie, le
Veil warlike arms from sight. Ye sons of Egypt dance a - round, And
sten - da sull' ar - mi un vel! Danziam, fan - ciul - le e - gi - zie,
Veil warlike arms from sight. Ye sons of E - gypt danc - ing,
mi - sti - che ca - ro - le, co - me d'in - tor - no al
sing your mys - tic prais - es, As round the sun in
le mi - sti - che ca - ro - le, co - me d'in -
Now sing your mys - tic prais - es, As round the
cresc.

so - - - - le dan - za - no gli a - strì in ciel.
maz - - - - es Dance all the stars in de - light.
tor - no al so - le dan - za - no gli a - strì in ciel.
sun in maz - es Danc - ing the stars de - light.
Chorus of Priests.
TENOR I.
TENOR II.
BASS I.
BASS II.
Del - la vit - to - ria a - gl'ar - bi - tri su - pre - mi il
Un - to the pow - er, war's is - sue dread de - cid - ing,
Del - la vit -
Un - to the
to - ria a - gl'ar - bi - tri su - pre - mi il
pow - er, war's is - sue dread de - cid - ing, our
Del - la vit -
Un - to the
guar - do er - ge - te,
Our glanc - es raise we,

f
Gra - zie a - gli
Thank we our
guar - do er - ge - te,
glanc - es up - raise we,
to - ria a - gl'ar - bi - tri su - pre - mi il
pow - er, war's is - sue dread de - cid - ing, Our
gra - zie a - gli Dei ren - de - te nel for - tu -
Thank we our gods, and praise we On this tri -
Dei ren - de - te nel
gods and praise we on
gra - zie a - gli Dei ren - de - te nel for - tu -
Thank we our gods, and praise we on this tri -
guar - do il guar - do er - get - te; gra - zie ren - de - te
glanc - es, our glanc - es raise we; Thank we and praise we
na - to di, gra - zie a - gli Dei, gra - zie ren - de - te nel
umphant day, Thank we our gods, thank we and praise we on

Chorus of People.
SOPRANO I.
ff
Co - me d'in - tor - no al
As round the Sun in
SOPRANO II.
ff
Co - me d'in - tor - no al
As round the Sun in
TENOR.
ff
In - ni fe -
Raise we our
BASS.
ff
In - ni fe -
Raise we our
Chorus of Priests.
for - tu - na - to dì, gra - zie a - gli
this tri - um - phant day, thank we the
na - to dì, gra - zie a - gli
um - phant day, thank we the
nel for - tu - na - to dì, gra - zie a - gli
On this tri - um - phant day, thank we the
for - tu - na - to dì, gra - zie a - gli
this tri - um - phant day, thank we the
ff

so - - le dan-za-no gli a-stri in ciel!
maz - - es Dance all the stars in de - light!
so - - le dan-za-no gli a-stri in ciel!
maz - - es Dance all the stars in de - light!
sto- si alziam al Re, al - zia - mo al Re.
fes - tal song, Raise we our song to the King.
sto- si alziam al Re, al - zia - mo al Re.
fes - tal song, Raise we our song to the King.
Dei ren- de - te nel for- tu- na - to dì.
gods and praise we On this tri-umphant day.
Dei ren- de - te nel for- tu- na - to dì.
gods and praise we On this tri-umphant day.
Dei ren- de - te nel for- tu- na - to dì.
gods and praise we On this tri-umphant day.
Dei ren- de - te nel for- tu- na - to dì.
gods and praise we On this tri-umphant day.
(The Egyptian troops, preceded by trumpets, defile before the King.)
mf

p
f
ff
mf

cresc.
Ballabile.
Più mosso. (♩ = 144)
p staccato
(A group of dancing-girls appears, bringing the spoils of the conquered)

mf
pp
ff
ff
pp

tr
f
pp
fz
p

fz
p
p
pp
mf
ff
p
pp
mf
ff

f
pp
m.s.
pp
pp
pp
ff
ppp

8
ff
pppp
pp
8
pp
8
f
ff

ff
ff
m.s.

f

pp
pp
fz
p
fz
p
fz
pp
fz
p
staccato e pp

mf
pp
ff

(Other troops enter, following war-chariots, banners, sacred vessels and images of the gods.)

noi;... sul pas - so de-gli e - ro - i, sul pas - so de - gli e-
ours;... Green bays and fra-grant flow-ers, Green bays and fra - grant
il guar - do er-ge - te, il guar - do er-ge-te,
our glanc - es raise we, our glanc - es raise we,
ff

Più animato.
ro - - i i lau - ri, i fior ver - siam!
flow- - ers Scat - ter their path a - long!
ro - - i i lau - ri, i fior ver - siam!
flow- - ers Scat - ter their path a - long!
ro - i i lau - ri, i fior ver - siam!
flow - ers Scat - ter their path a - long!
ro- - i i lau - ri, i fior ver - siam!
flow- - ers Scat - ter their path a - long!
il guar - do er - ge - te;
Our glanc - es raise we;
il guar - do er - ge - te;
Our glanc - es raise we;
il guar - do er - ge - te;
Our glanc - es raise we;
il guar - do er - ge - te;
Our glanc - es raise we;
Più animato. (♩ = 132)
mf

Priests.
gra - zie a - gli Dei, a - gli Dei ren -
Thank we our gods, thank our gods and
gra - zie a - gli Dei, a - gli Dei ren -
Thank we our gods, thank our gods and
gra - zie a - gli Dei, a - gli Dei ren -
Thank we our gods, thank our gods and
de - te nel for - tu - na - to dì.
praise we On this tri - um - phant day.
de - te nel for - tu - na - to dì.
praise we On this tri - um - phant day.
de - te nel for - tu - na - to
praise we On this tri - um - phant

People.
Vie - ni, o guerrier, vie - ni a gio - ir, a gio-ir con noi, o guer -
Hith - er, glorious band, min - gle your joy, mingle your joy with ours, hith - er ad -
Glo - ria, glo - ria, glo - ria, glo - ria al guer.
Glo - ry, glo - ry, glo - ry, glo - ry be
Glo - ria, glo - ria, glo - ria, glo - ria al guer.
Glo - ry, glo - ry, glo - ry, glo - ry be
Priests.
Gra - zie, gra - zie, gra - zie, gra - zie a - gli
Thank we, thank we, thank we, thank we our
Gra - zie, gra - zie, gra - zie, gra - zie a - gli
Thank we, thank we, thank we, thank we our
dì. Gra - zie, gra - zie, gra - zie, gra - zie a - gli
day. Thank we, thank we, thank we, thank we our

ff stent.
rier, vie - ni o guer - rier, vie - ni a gio - ir con noi, vie - ni,
vance, oh glo - rious band, Min - gle your joy with ours, hith - er,
rier, glo - ria al guer - rier, vie - ni, vie - ni,
yours, glo - ry be yours, hith - er, hith - er,
rier, glo - ria al guer - rier, vie - ni, vie - ni,
yours, glo - ry be yours, hith - er, hith - er,
rier, glo - ria al guer - rier, vie - ni, o guer - rier, vie - ni,
yours, glo - ry be yours, hith - er, glorious band, hith - er,
Dei, gra - zie a - gli Dei ren - de - te, gra - zie
gods, thank we our gods, and praise we, thank our
Dei, gra - zie a - gli Dei ren - de - te, gra - zie
gods, thank we our gods, and praise we, thank our
Dei, gra - zie a - gli Dei ren - de - te, gra - zie
gods, thank we our gods, and praise we, thank our
Dei, gra - zie a - gli Dei ren - de - te, gra - zie
gods, thank we our gods, and praise we, thank our
ff stent.

ritenuto come prima
ff
vie - ni, vie - ni, o guer - rier, vie-ni a gio - ir con
hith - er, hith - er, glo - rious band, Mingle your joy, your
o guer - rie - ro, vie - ni, o guer - rier, vie-ni a gio - ir con
glorious warriors, hith - er, glo - rious band, Mingle your joy, your
a - gli De - i,
gods and praise we,
ff riten. come prima

no - i, sul pas - so de - gl'e - ro - ij lau-ri e i fior ver-
joy with ours, Green bays and fra-grant flow - ers We'll scat - ter on their
no - i, sul pas - so de - gl'e - ro - ij lau-ri e i fior ver-
joy with ours, Green bays and fra-grant flow - ers We'll scat - ter on their
no - i, sul pas - so de - gl'e - ro - ij lau-ri e i fior ver-
joy with ours, Green bays and fra-grant flow - ers We'll scat - ter on their
ff
gra-zie a-gli Dei,
thank we our gods,
ff
gra-zie a-gli Dei,
thank we our gods,
ff
gra-zie a-gli Dei,
thank we our gods,
ff

siam. Vie - ni, o guer - rie - o, vie - ni a gio - ir con
path. Hith - er ad - vance, glo - rious band, Min - gle your joy with
siam. Vie - ni, o guer - rie - o, vie - ni a gio - ir con
path. Hith - er ad - vance, glo - rious band, Min - gle your joy with
siam. Vie - ni, o guer - rie - o, vie - ni a gio - ir con
path. Hith - er ad - vance, glo - rious band, Min - gle your joy with
gra-zie a-gli Dei, gra - zie a-gli Dei
thank we our gods, thank we our gods
gra-zie a-gli Dei, gra - zie a-gli Dei
thank we our gods, thank we our gods
gra-zie a-gli Dei, gra - zie a-gli Dei
thank we our gods, thank we our gods

noi; sul pas-so de-gl'e-ro-i i lauri, i fior ver-
ours; Green bays and fragrant flow-ers We'll scatter their path a-
noi; sul pas-so de-gl'e-ro-i i lauri, i fior ver-
ours; Green bays and fragrant flow-ers We'll scatter their path a-
noi; sul pas-so de-gl'e-ro-i i lauri, i fior ver-
ours; Green bays and fragrant flow-ers We'll scatter their path a-
noi; sul pas-so de-gl'e-roi-i lauri, i fior ver-
ours; Green bays and fragrant flow-ers Scatter their path a-
ren-de-te, grazie a-gli Dei ren-de-te,
and praise we, yes, thank our gods and praise we,
ren-de-te, grazie a-gli Dei ren-de-te,
and praise we, yes, thank our gods and praise we,
ren-de-te, grazie a-gli Dei ren-de-te,
and praise we, yes, thank our gods and praise we,

(Enter Radamès under a canopy carried by twelve officers.)

ria! glo - - ria, glo - ria al-l'E-git-to, glo - -
ry! glo - - ry, glo - ry to E-gypt, glo - -
ria! glo - - ria, glo - ria al-l'E-git-to, glo - -
ry! glo - - ry, glo - ry to E-gypt, glo - -
ria! glo - - ria, glo - ria al-l'E-git-to, glo - -
ry! glo - - ry, glo - ry to E-gypt, glo - -
ria! glo - - ria, glo - ria al-l'E-git-to, glo - -
ry! glo - - ry, glo - ry to E-gypt, glo - -
de - te nel for-tu-na-to dì, gra - zia a-gli
praise we on this tri-um-phant day, thank we our
de - te nel for-tu-na-to dì, gra - zia a-gli
praise we on this tri-um-phant day, thank we our
de - te nel for-tu-na-to dì, gra - zia a-gli
praise we on this tri-um-phant day, thank we our
de - te nel for-tu-na-to dì, gra - zia a-gli
praise we on this tri-um-phant day, thank we our

ria, glo - ria al - l'E - git - to, glo - - ria, glo - -
ry, glo - ry to E - gypt, glo - - ry, glo - -
ria, glo - ria al - l'E - git - to, glo - - ria, glo - ria
ry, glo - ry to E - gypt, glo - - ry, glo - ry
ria, glo - ria al - l'E - git - to, glo - - ria, glo - -
ry, glo - ry to E - gypt, glo - - ry, glo - -
ria, glo - ria al - l'E - git - to, glo - - ria, glo - -
ry, glo - ry to E - gypt, glo - - ry, glo - -
Dei, gra - zia a - gli Dei, gra - -
gods, thank we our gods, thank
Dei, gra - zia a - gli Dei, gra - -
gods, thank we our gods, thank
Dei, gra - zia a - gli Dei, gra - -
gods, thank we our gods, thank
Dei, gra - zia a - gli Dei, gra - -
gods, thank we our gods, thank

glo - - - ria, glo - ria, glo - - -
glo - - - ry, glo - ry, glo - - -
ria, glo - - ria, glo - ria, glo - - -
ry, glo - - ry, glo - - ry, glo - - - -
- - - - - ria, glo - - -
- - - - - ry, glo - - -
- - - - - zie a - gli
we our
zie, gra - zie, gra - zie ren - de - te a - gli
we, thank we, thank we and praise we our
zie, gra - zie, gra - zie ren - de - te a - gli
we, thank we, thank we and praise we our
zie, gra - zie, gra - zie ren - de - te a gli
we, thank we, thank we and praise we our

(**The King descends from** the throne to embrace Radamès.)

The King.
Sal-va-tor del-la pa-tria, io ti sa-lu - - - to!
Savior brave of thy country, E-gypt sa-lutes thee!
col canto
ff
Vieni, e mia fi-glia di sua man ti por-ga il ser-to tri-on-
Hither now ad-vance, and on thy head my daughter will place the crown of
p
(Radamès bends before Amneris, who hands him the crown.)
fa-le.
triumph.
ff
Come prima. (♩= 92.)
ppp
(to Radamès.)
O-ra a me chie-di quan-to più bra-mi. Nul-la a te ne-
What boon thou ask-est, free-ly I'll grant it. Naught can be de-
p

ga - to sarà in tal dì - lo giu - ro per la co - ro - na mi - a, pei sa - cri
nied thee on such a day. I swear it by the crown I am wearing, by heav'n a -
mf
Radamès.
Poco più.
Con - ce - di in pria che innan - zi a te sien trat - ti i pri - gio - nier. -
First deign to or - der that the captives be be - fore you brought.
Nu - mi!
bove us!
Poco più. (♩=100)
pp
pp
(Enter Ethiopian prisoners surrounded by guards, Amonasro last in the dress of an officer.)
Ramphis.
ppp
p
Gra - zie a - gli De - i, gra - zie ren - de -
Thank we our gods, thank our gods and praise
TENORS.
Priests.
Gra - zie a - gli De - i, gra - zie ren - de -
Thank we our gods, thank our gods and praise
BASSES.
Gra - zie a - gli De - i, gra - zie ren - de -
Thank we our gods, thank our gods and praise
ppp

te nel— for-tu - na - to, nel— for-tu-na-to—
we on— this tri - umph - ant, on— this triumph-ant—
te nel— for-tu - na - to, nel— for-tu-na-to—
we on— this tri - umph - ant, on— this tri-umph-ant—
te nel— for-tu - na - to, nel— for-tu-na-to—
we on— this tri - umph - ant, on— this tri-umph-ant—
morendo
pp
dì, gra-zie, gra-zie a-gli Dei.
day, all thanks, all thanks to our gods.
pp
dì, gra-zie, gra-zie a-gli Dei.
day, all thanks, all thanks to our gods.
pp
dì, gra-zie, gra-zie a-gli Dei.
day, all thanks, all thanks to our gods.
ancora più p
pp

Allegro assai vivo.
Aïda.
(Rushing towards Amonasro.)
Che veg-go!... E-gli?... Mio pa-dre!...
What see I?... he here!... My fa-ther!...
Amneris.
Suo pa - - dre!
Her fa - - ther!
Radamès.
Suo pa - - dre!
Her fa - - ther!
Ramphis.
Suo pa - - dre!
Her fa - - ther!
The King.
Suo pa - - dre!
Her fa - - ther!
Priests.
TENORS.
Suo pa - - dre!
Her fa - - ther!
BASSES.
Suo pa - - dre!
Her fa - - ther!
People.
SOPRANOS.
Suo pa - - dre!
Her fa - - ther!
TENORS.
Suo pa - - dre!
Her fa - - ther!
BASSES.
Allegro assai vivo. (𝅗𝅥 = 144.)
f
ff

Aïda.
(Embracing her father.)
Tu! pri-gio - nier!
Thou! captive made!
Amneris.
In po-ter no-stro!
And in our pow-er!
Amonasro.
(whispering to Aida.)
Non mi tra-dir!
Tell not my rank!
mf
f
The King.
(to Amonasro.)
T'ap - pres - sa.
Come for-ward.
ff
f
ff
Amonasro.
Molto largo.
p
Suo pa - dre. An-ch'io pu-
Her fa - ther. I too have
Dun - que tu sei?
So then thou art?
Molto largo. (♩ = 52.)
pp
gnai vin-ti noi fum-mo mor-te in-van cer - cai.
fought and we are conquer'd death I vain-ly sought.
ppp
pppp

Andante sostenuto. (♩ = 66.)
(pointing to the uniform he is wearing.)
Amonasro.
Que-st'às-si - sa ch'io ve-sto vi di - ca che il mio
This my gar - ment has told you al-read - y that I
pp
Re, la mia patria ho di - fe - so; fu la
fought to de-fend King and coun-try; Adverse
ff
pp
sor - te a nostr'ar - mi ne-mi - ca__ tor-nò va - no de' for - ti l'ar-
for - tune against us ran stea - dy__ Vain-ly sought we the fates to de -
dir. Al mio piè _ nel-la pol - ve di - ste-so giac-que il
fy. At my feet _ in the dust _ lay ex-tend-ed Our
ff
pp
f

Re — da più col - pi tra - fit - to; se l'a - mor del - la
King, — countless wounds had trans - pierc'd him; If to fight for the
f
cresc.
pa - tria è de - lit - to siam rei
coun - try that — nurs'd him Make one
tronca
Poco più animato. (♩ = 76.)
tut - ti, siam pronti a mo - rir! Ma tu, Re, tu si - gno - re pos -
guil - ty, we're read - y to die! But, oh King, in thy pow - er trans -
f
pppp legato
dolce
sen - te, a co - sto - ro ti vol - gi cle - men - te — Og - gi
cen - dent, Spare the lives on thy mer - cy de - pen - dent — By the

ten.
noi siam per-cos-si dal fa-to, ah! do-man voi po-tria il fa-to col-
fates though to-day o-ver-tak-en, Ah! say__ who can to-morrow's e-vent de-
ten.
p
Aïda.
p
Ma tu Re, tu si-gno-re pos-sen-te, a co-
But, oh King, in thy pow-er tran-scen-dent Spare the
pir.
scry?
Slave-prisoners.
p
Sì: dai Nu-mi per-cos-si noi sia-mo; tua pie-
We, on whom heav-en's an-ger is fall-ing, Thee im-
p
Sì: dai Nu-mi per-cos-si noi sia-mo; tua pie-
We, on whom heav-en's an-ger is fall-ing, Thee im-
sempre legato
sto-ro ti vol-gi cle-men-te, Og-gi noi siam per-cos-si dal
lives on thy mer-cy de-pen-dent, By the fates tho' to day o-ver-
p
tà, tua cle-men-za im-plo-ria-mo; ah giam-mai di sof-frir vi sia
plore, on thy clem-en-cy call-ing; May ye ne'er be by for-tune for-
p
tà, tua cle-men-za im-plo-ria-mo; ah giam-mai di sof-frir vi sia
plore, on thy clem-en-cy call-ing; May ye ne'er be by for-tune for-
p

fa - to, ah! do - man voi po - tria il fa - to col - pir.
tak - en, Ah! say, who can to-morrow's e - vent de - sery?
Amonasro.
Ah! do - man voi po - tria il fa - to col - pir.
Ramphis. Ah! say, who can to-morrow's e - vent de - sery?
Strug - gi o
Death, oh
Slave-prisoners.
da - to ciò che in og - gi n'è da - to sof - frir!
sak - en, Nor like us in cap - tiv - i - ty lie!
ciò che in og - gi n'è da - to sof - frir!
Nor like us in cap - tiv - i - ty lie!
da - to ciò che n'è da - to sof - frir!
sak - en, Nor thus in cap-tiv - i - ty lie!
Priests.
Strug - gi o
Death, oh
Strug - gi o
Death, oh
Ramphis.
Re, que - ste ciur - me fe - ro - ci, chiu - di il
King, be their just des - ti - na - tion, Close thy
Priests.
Re, que - ste ciur - me fe - ro - ci, chiu - di il
King, be their just des - ti - na - tion, Close thy
Re, que - ste ciur - me fe - ro - ci, chiu - di il
King, be their just des - ti - na - tion, Close thy

Aïda.
Pie - tà!
Ah spare!
Ramphis.
cor al - le per - fi - de vo - ci; fur dai
heart to all vain sup - pli - ca - tion, By the
Slave-prisoners.
Priests.
m.s.
m.d.
pie - tà!
ah spare!
Nu - mi vo - ta - ti al - la mor - te, or de'
heav - ens they doom'd are to per - ish, We the

13573

string. a poco a poco
pie - tà! Ma_ tu, o Re, si - gnor pos -
ah spare! But_ thou, oh King, in thy pow'r trans -
Amneris.
Qua - li sguardi,_ qua - li sguardi_
With what glances,_ with what glances_
Amonasro.
Og - gi no - i siam per - cos -
By the fates_ tho' we to - day_
Ramphis.
con forza
Nu - - mi si compia il vo - ler! A mor - te! a
heav - - ens are bound to o - bey! To death all! to
The King.
Or che fau - sti ne ar - ri -
High in tri - umph since our ban -
Slave-prisoners.
pie - tà! tua pie - ta - de, tua cle - men -
ah spare! we im - plore_ thee, on thy clem -
pie - tà! tua pie - ta - de, tua cle - men -
ah spare! we im - plore_ thee, on thy clem -
Priests.
Nu - - mi si compia il vo - ler! A mor - te! a
heav - - ens are bound to o - bey! To death all! to
con forza
Nu - - mi si compia il vo - ler! A mor - te! a
heav - - ens are bound to o - bey! To death all! to
People.
SOPRANOS.
Sa - cer - do - ti, gli sde -
Ho - ly priests, calm your_ an -
TENOR.
Sa - cer - do - ti, gli sde -
Ho - ly priests, calm your an -
BASS.
m.s. m.d.
string. a poco a poco

ff
sen - te, a co - sto - ro ti mo - stra cle - men - - -
cen - dent, spare the lives on thy mer - cy de - pen - - -
so-vr'es-sa ha ri - vol - ti! di qual fiam - ma ba -
on her he is gaz - ing! glow-ing pas - sion with-
si dal fa - to, voi do - man po-tria il
are o - ver - ta'en, who the e - vent can of to-
mor - te! a mor - te! o Re, struggi,
death all! to death all! oh King, now be
don gli e - ven - ti a co - sto - ro mostriam-ci cle-
ners now are soar - ing, Let us spare those our mer - cy im-
za im - plo - ria - mo, ah pie -
en - cy now call - ing, spare us
za im - plo - ria - mo, tua cle -
en - cy now call - ing, on thy
mor - te! a mor - te! o Re, struggi,
death all! to death all! oh King, now be
mor - te! a mor - te! o Re, struggi,
death all! to death all! oh King, now be
gni pla - ca - te, l'u - mil
ger ex - ceed - ing, lend an
gni pla - ca - te, l'u - mil
ger ex - ceed - ing, lend an
ff

te.
dent.
cupo
le - na-noi vol - ti! quali sguardi sovr'essa hari-
in them is blaz - ing! With what glances on her he is
Radamès.
(fixing his eyes on Aida)
pp
(Il do - lor che in quel vol - to fa-
(See her cheek wan with weep - ing and
pp
fa - to col - pir. Tua pie-
mor - row de - scry. We im-
strug-gi que-ste ciur - me,
death their des-ti - na - tion,
p
men - ti, or che
plor - ing, High in
tà, pie - tà,
we im - plore,
men - za jm-plo-ria - mo,
clem - en - cy call - ing,
strug-gi que-ste ciur - me,
death their des-ti - na - tion,
strug-gi que-ste ciur - me,
death their des-ti - na - tion,
pre - ce a scol-ta - te;
ear to their plead - ing;
pre - ce a scol-ta - te;
ear to their plead - ing;
pp dolce

p dolce
tua pie - tà im -
I im - plore thy
vol-ti! di qual fiamma ba-le - na - noi
gazing! Glowing passion with-in them is
vel - la al mio sguar - do la ren - de più
sor - row From af - flic - tion new charm seems to
tà, tua cle-men-za implo - ria-mo,
plore, on thy clemen-cy calling,
si com -
we of
fau - sti ne ar-ri - don gli e - ven - ti,
tri - umph our ban - ners are soar - ing,
pp
pie-tà,
ah spare,
pie-
ah
si com -
we of
sa-cer-do - ti, gli sdegni pla -
Ho-ly priests,calm your anger ex -
dolce
pp

plo - ro.
mer - cy.
vol - ti! Ed io so-la, av-vi-li-ta, re-
blaz - ing! She is lov'd, and my passion is
bel - la; o - gni stil - la del pian - to a - do -
bor - row; In my bo - som love's flame seems new -
tua pie -
we im -
pi-sca de' Nu-mi il vo-ler!
heav-en the will must o-bey!
a co -
spare, we
tà,
spare,
pi-sca de' Nu-mi il vo-ler!
heav-en the will must o-bey!
pi-sca de' Nu-mi il vo-ler!
heav-en the will must o-bey!
ca-te,
ceed-ing,
ca-te,
ceed-ing,

13573

jet-ta? la ven - det - ta mi rug - - ge nel
slighted? Stern re - venge in my breast loud-ly
ra - to nel mio pet - to rav - vi - va l'a -
light - ed by each tear - drop that flows from her
tà, tua cle - men - - za im - - plo -
plore, we thy mer - - cy im -
sto - ro mo-striam - ci cle - men - - -
those then our mer - cy im - plor - - -
ah, pie - tà,
we im - plore,
pie -
ah
pp
l'u - mil pre - ce de' vin - ti a - scol -
Lend an ear to the conquer'd foe
pp
l'u - mil pre - ce de' vin - ti a - scol -
Lend an ear to the conquer'd foe

og - gi no - i siam per-cos - si,
By fate tho' we're now o'er-tak - en,
cor, la ven - det - ta, la ven - det - ta
cries, stern-ly ven - geance, stern-ly ven - geance
mor, o - gni stil-la del pian - to a - do -
eyes, in my bosom love's flame seems new-
riam, tua clemenza implo-riam, tua clemenza implo -
plore, we thy mercy im - plore, we thy mercy im -
strug - gi, o Re, que-ste ciur - me, que - ste ciur-me fe - ro - ci,
death, oh King, yes, let death be now their just des-ti - na - tion,
ti: la pie - tà sa - le ai
ing: By the gods mer - cy
pie - tà, pie-
ah spare, ah
tà, tua clemenza implo-riam, tua clemenza implo -
spare, we thy mercy im - plore, we thy mer-cy im -
strug - gi, o Re, que-ste ciur - me, que - ste ciur-me fe - ro - ci,
Death, oh King, yes, let death be now their just des - ti - na - tion,
strug - gi, o Re, que-ste ciur - me, que - ste ciur-me fe - ro - ci,
Death, oh King, yes, let death be now their just des - ti - na - tion,
ta - te;
pleading;
ta - te;
pleading;

do - man voi po - tri - a
ah! say who to - mor - row's,
mi rug - ge, nel cor, mi
in my breast loud - ly cries, in my
ra - to, del pian - to a - do - ra - to nel mio pet - to,
kin - dled, love's flame seems new kin - dled by each tear - drop,
riam, im - plo - ria - mo, tua pie -
plore, we im - plore thee, we im -
strug - gi, strug - gi; fur dai Nu - mi vo -
let them per - ish; they are doom'd by the
Nu - mi gra - di - ta e raf - fer - ma,
aye is re - quit - ed and con - firm - eth,
tà, tua pie - ta - de,
spare, spare, oh spare us,
riam, tua pie - ta - de,
plore, spare, ah spare us,
strug - gi, strug - gi; fur dai Nu - mi vo -
death all, death all; they are doom'd by the
strug - gi, strug - gi; fur dai Nu - mi vo -
let them per - ish; they are doom'd by the
sa - cer - do - ti,
Ho - ly priest - hood,
People.
sa - cer - do - ti,
Ho - ly priest - hood,
sa - cer - do - ti,
Ho - ly priest - hood,

po - tri - a il fa - to
to - mor - row's e - vent can
rug - ge nel co - re,
breast loud ven - geance cry - eth,
nel mio pet - to rav - vi - va
by each tear - drop that flows from
ta - de, tua cle - men - za
plore thee, we for mer - cy
ta - ti, fur vo - ta - ti al la mor - te, si com - pi - sca de'
heav - ens, they are doom'd all to per - ish, and the will of the
e raf - fer - ma il po - ter,
and con - firm - eth prince - ly sway,
tua cle - men - za in - vo - chia - mo,
we for mer - cy all im - plore thee,
tua cle - men - za in - vo - chiam,
we for mer - cy thee im - plore,
ta - ti, vo - ta - ti al - la mor - te, si com - pi - sca de'
heav - ens, they are doom'd all to per - ish, and the will of the
ta - ti, vo - ta - ti al - la mor - te, si com - pi - sca de'
heav - ens, they are doom'd all to per - ish, and the will of the
gli sde - gni pla - ca - te,
calm your an - ger ex - ceed - ing,
gli sde - gni pla - ca - te,
calm your an - ger ex - ceed - ing,
gli sde - gni pla - ca - te,
calm your an - ger ex - ceed - ing,

ff
dim.
allarg.
pp a tempo.
col - pir. Ma tu, o
des - cry. But, oh
pp
nel cor. Ed io
loud cries. She is
pp
l'ar - dor, Il do -
her eyes, Her fair
pp
im - plo - riam. Ma tu, o
thee im - plore. But, oh
pp
Nu - mi, de' Nu - mi il vo - ler! Strug - gi, o Re, que - ste
heav - ens we all must o - bey! Death, oh King, yes, let
pp
il po - ter. La
prince - ly sway. Mer -
pp
in - vo - chaim. Sì dai
we im - plore. We on
pp
in - vo - chaim. Sì dai
we im - plore. We on
Nu - mi, de' Nu - mi il vo - ler!
heav - ens we must all o - bey!
cupo
pp
Nu - mi, de' Nu - mi il vo - ler! Strug - gi, o Re, que - ste
heav - ens we must all o - bey! Death, oh King, yes, let
pp
pie - tà! Re pos -
ah spare! King, we
pp
pie - tà! Re
ah spare! King,
pp
pp legato

Re, tu si - gno - re pos - sen - te, a co - -
King, in thy pow - er tran - scend - ent Spare the
so-la, av- - vi - li - ta, av - vi -
loved and my passion, and my
lor, il do - lor
cheek, her fair cheek
Re, tu si - gno - re pos - sen - te, a co - -
King, in thy pow - er tran - scend - ent Spare the
ciur - me, que-ste ciurme fe - ro - ci, fur dai Nu-mi vo -
death be their most just desti - na - tion, they by heaven are
pie - tà,
- - cy, aye,
Nu - mi per - cos - si noi sia - mo, tua pie -
whom heav - en's an - ger is fall - ing thee im -
Nu - mi per - cos - si noi sia - mo, tua pie -
whom heav - en's an - ger is fall - ing thee im -
pp
Struggi, o Re, ques-te ciur - me, que-ste ciurme fe-ro-ci,
Death, oh King, yes, let death be their just desti-na-tion,
ciur - me que-ste ciurme fe - ro - ci, fur dai Nu-mi vo -
death be their most just desti - na - tion, they by heaven are
sen - te,
cher - ish,
pos - sen - te,
we cher - ish,

sto - ro ti mo - stra cle - men - te_ og - gi
lives on thy mer - cy de - pend - ent,_ By the
li-ta, re - jet - ta? la ven-
passion is slight - ed? stern-ly
la_
seems_
sto - ro ti mo - stra cle - men - te_ og - gi
lives on thy mer - cy de - pend - ent,_ By the
ta - ti, fur vo - ta-ti alla mor - te, si com-pi - sca de'
fat - ed, they are fat-ed to per - ish, And the heavens we
la_
mer -
tà, tua ele - men - za im-plo - ria - mo: ah! giam-
plore, on thy clem - en - cy call - ing; May ye
tà, tua ele - men - za im-plo - ria - mo: ah! giam-
plore, on thy clem - en - cy call - ing; May ye
fur dai Nu-mi vo - ta - ti, fur vo-ta-ti al-la morte,
they by heav-en are fat-ed, they are fat-ed to per-ish,
ta - ti, fur vo - ta-ti alla mor - te, si com-pi - sca de'
fat - ed, they are fat-ed to per - ish, and the heav-ens we
Re pos -
King we
Re pos -
King we
pp

noi siam per - cos - si dal fa - to, ah do - man voi potria il fato col -
fates tho' to - day o - ver - tak - en, Ah, say who can to-morrow's event des -
detta mi rug - ge nel cor.
vengeance with-in loud-ly cries.
ren - de più bel - la;
new charm to bor - row;
noi siam per - cos - si dal fa - to, ah do - man voi potria il fa - to col -
fates tho' to - day o - ver - tak - en, Ah, say who can to-morrow's e - vent des-
Nu - mi, si com - pi - sca de' Nu - mi il vo - ler!
all, and the heavens we all must o - bey!
pie - tà,
- cy, aye,
mai di sof - frir vi sia da - to ciò che in og - gi n'è da - to sof-
ne'er be by for - tune for - sak - en, Nor e'er like us in cap - tiv - i - ty
ciò che in og - gi n'è da - to sof-
Nor e'er like us in cap - tiv - i - ty
mai di sof - frir vi sia da - to ciò che n'è da - to sof-
ne'er be by for - tune for sak - en, e'er in cap - tiv - i - ty
si com - pi - sca de' Nu - mi il vo - ler!
and the heavens we all must, must o - bey!
Nu - mi si com - pi - sca de' Numi il vo - ler!
all, and the heav - ens we all must o - bey!
sen - te,
cher - ish,
sen - te,
cher - ish,
ten.
p

pir, do-man voi, do-man voi il
cry, who to-morrow's, who to-morrow's e-
ed io so-la, av-vi-li-ta, av-vi-
She is lov-ed, and my passion, and my
o-gni stil-la, o-gni stil-la del
in my bo-som, in my bo-som love's
pir, og-gi no-i, og-gi no-i siam per-
cry, By the fates, by the fates we're to-
struggi,o Re, struggi,o Re, que-ste ciurme,
death, oh King, death, oh King, let them perish,
la pie-tà, la pie-tà sa-le ai
mer-cy, aye, mer-cy, aye by the
frir! ah giam-ma-i, ah giam-ma-i di sof-
lie! may you nev-er, may you nev-er be by
frir! ah giam-ma-i, ah giam-ma-i di sof-
lie! may you nev-er, may you nev-er be by
struggi,o Re, struggi,o Re que-ste ciurme,
death, oh King, death, oh King, let them perish,
struggi,o Re, struggi,o Re que-ste ciurme,
death, oh King, death, oh King, let them perish,
e tu,o Re, tu, o Re, tu pos-
mighty King, mighty King, thou whose
e tu,o Re, tu, o Re, tu pos-
mighty King, mighty King, thou whose

ff
fa - - - - - - - - - - - - - - to po -
vent can, to
li - - ta, re - jet - - - - - ta? la ven -
pas - - sion is slight - - - - - ed? Stern ly
pian - to a - do - ra - to nel mio pet - to, nel mio
flame seems new - light - ed By each tear - drop, by each
cos - - si dal fa - to, voi do - -
day o - ver - tak - en, Yet who
fur dai Nu - mi vo - ta - - ti al - la mor - te,
they by heav - en are fat - - ed to per - ish,
Nu - - mi gra - di - ta e raf - -
gods is re - quit - ed, And of
frir vi sia da - to ciò che in og - gi, ciò che in
for - - tune for - sak - en, Nor like us, nor e'er like
frir vi sia da - to ciò che in og - gi, ciò che in
for - - tune for - sak - en, Nor like us, nor e'er like
fur dai Nu - mi vo - ta - - ti al - la mor - te,
they by heav - en are fat - - ed to per - ish,
fur dai Nu - mi vo - ta - - ti al - la mor - te,
they by heav - en are fat - - ed to per - ish,
sen - - te, tu for - te, a cle - men - za a cle -
pow - - er we cher - ish, in thy bo - som let
sen - - te, tu for - te, a cle - men - za a cle -
pow - - er we cher - ish, in thy bo - som let
ff

mf string.
tri - a doman vo - i potria col - pir, do - man
mor - row's, can to - mor - row's e - vent des - cry, say, who
det - ta la ven - det - ta rugge nel cor, la ven-
ven - geance, stern - ly ven - geance within me cries, yes, stern-
pet - to rav - vi - va l'ar - dor, nel mio
tear - drop that flows from her eyes, by each,
man il fa - to po - tri - a col - pir, do - man
can to - mor - row's e - vent e'er des - cry, yes, who
pp
si compi - sca de' Nu - mi il voler! fur dai Nu - mi, dai
we of heav - en the will must o - bey, they by heav - en, by
fer - ma de' pren - ci il po - ter,
princ - es it strength - ens the sway,
og - gi n'è da - to sof - frir!
us in cap - tiv - i - ty lie!
og - gi n'è
us in cap -
og - gi n'è da - to sof - frir!
us in cap - tiv - i - ty lie!
pp string.
si compi - sca de' Nu - mi il voler! fur dai Nu - mi, dai
we of heav - en the will must o - bey! they by heav - en, by
pp
si compi - sca de' Nu - mi il voler! fur dai Nu - mi, dai
we of heav - en the will must o - bey! they by heav - en, by
men - za di - schiudi il pen - sier,
mer - cy, let mer - cy have sway,
men - za di - schiu - di il pen - sier,
mer - cy, let mer - cy have sway,
men - za di schiu - di il pen - sier,
mer - cy, let mer - cy have sway,
8
string.
ppp

a poco a poco
ff
voi potria il fa-to, do-man voi po-tria col-pir,
can des-cry, to-morrow, who to-morrow, can des-cry,
det-ta, la ven-det-ta, la ven-det-ta rug-ge, rugge in cor,
ven-geance, yes, stern vengeance, yes, stern vengeance loud with-in me cries,
pet-to, nel mio pet-to o-gni stil-la del suo pian-to,
each teardrop, each teardrop, in my bo-som love is light-ed,
voi po-tria il fa-to, do-man voi po-tria col-pi-re,
can, who can to-morrow e'er des-cry, des-cry, to mor-row,
Nu-mi vo-ta-ti al-la morte, fur vo-ta-ti al-la mor-te,
heav-en are fat-ed to perish, they are fat-ed all to per-ish,
ai Nu-mi sa-le gra-di-ta,
aye by the gods is re-quit-ed,
ah, tua cle-men-za im-plo-ria-mo,
ah, see for mer-cy we im-plore thee,
a poco a poco
Nu-mi vo-ta-ti al-la mor-te, fur vo-ta-ti al-la mor-te,
heav-en are fat-ed to perish, they are fat-ed all to per-ish,
a cle-men-za di-schiu-di il pen-sier,
ah, let mer-cy, let mer-cy have sway,
ff

Come prima.
pp
voi po-tria col - pir
say who can des - cry.
pp
rug - - ge in cor, in
loud - - ly cries, loud
pp
nel mio pet - to rav-vi - va l'ar-dor, l'ar -
by each tear - drop that flows from her eyes, her
pp
do-man voi po-tria col-pir, po-tria col -
who to-mor - row can des-cry, who can des -
p
si compi-sca de' Numi il vo-ler, de' Nu-mi il vo-
we of heaven the will must o - bey, the heavens o-
p
e raf-fer - ma il po-ter, raf-fer-ma il po-
and confirm - eth the sway, of princes the
pp
im - - plo-riam, im - plo-
we im-plore, we im-
pp
im - - plo-riam, im - plo-
we im-plore, we im-
p allarg.
si compi-sca de' Nu-mi il vo-ler, de' Nu-mi il vo-
we of heaven the will must o - bey, the heavens o-
p
si compi-sca de' Nu-mi il vo-ler, de' Nu-mi il vo-
we of heaven the will must o - bey, the heavens o-
pp
o Re po-sen-te
oh King, al-might-y
pp
o Re po-sen-te
oh King, al-might-y
pp
Come prima.
ppp
ppp
ppp

Allegro
cor.
cries.
Recit.
dor,
eyes,
O Re: pei sa - cri Nu-mi, per lo splen-dor del-la tua co-
O King: by heav'n a - bove us, and by the crown on thy brow thou
pir.
cry?
ler!
bey!
ter.
sway.
riam.
plore.
riam.
plore.
ler.
bey.
ler.
bey.
Re.
King.
Re.
King.
Allegro (♩=120)
ff
p

13578

Radamès.
ro - na, com-pier giu - ra - sti il vo - to mi - o. Eb -
swor - est, what-e'er I asked thee thou wouldst grant it. Vouch -
King.
Giurai.
Say on.
Radamès.
be - ne: a te pei pri - gio - nie - ri E - ti - o - pi vi - ta do -
safe then, I pray free-dom and life to free - ly grant un - to these
p
Amneris.
(Per tut-ti!)
(Free all, then!)
Radamès.
man - do e li - ber - tà.
E - thiop cap-tives here.
Priests.
f
Mor - te ai ne - mi - ci del - la
Death be the doom of E - gypt's
f
Mor - te ai ne - mi - ci del - la
Death be the doom of E - gypt's
f

Ramphis.
Ascol-ta, o
Hear me, oh
Priests.
pa-tri-a!
en-e-mies!
pa-tri-a!
en-e-mies!
People.
pp
Gra-zia per gl'in-fe-li-ci!
Com-pas-sion to the wretch-ed!
Gra-zia per gl'in-fe-li-ci!
Com-pas-sion to the wretch-ed!
(to Radamès.)
Re. Tu pu-re gio-vi-ne e-ro-e, sag-gio con-si-glio a-
King! and thou, too, daunt-less young he-ro, lost to the voice of
a tempo (♩= 88)
scol-ta: son ne-mi-ci e pro-di so-no la ven-det-ta han-no nel
pru-dence: they are foes, to bat-tle hard-ened, Vengeance ne'er in them will

cor, fat-ti au-da-ci dal per-do-no cor-re-ran-no all' ar-mi an-
die, Grow-ing bold-er if now par-don'd, They to arms once more will
Radamès.
Spen-to A-mo-na-sro il re guer-rier, non re-sta speran-za ai vin-ti.
With A-mo-nas-ro, their warrior King, all hopes of revenge have perish'd.
cor!
fly!
p
Ramphis.
Al-me-no, ar-ra di pa-ce e se-cur-tà, fra noi re-sti col pa-dre A-
At least, as earnest of safe-ty and of peace, Keep we back then A-i-da's
pp legato
i-da...
fa-ther.
The King.
Al tuo consiglio io ce-do. Di se-cur-tà, di pa-ce un mi-glior pe-gno or io vo'
I yield me to thy counsel; of safe-ty now and peace a bond more certain will I

Più presto.(𝅗𝅥 = 120.)
dar-vi. Radamès, la pa-tria tutto a te de-ve.
give you. Radamès, to thee ourdebt is un-bounded.
ff
D'Am-ne-ris, la ma-no pre-mio ti
Am-ne-ris, my daugh-ter, shall be thy
p string.
si-a. So-vra l'E-git-to un gior-no con
guer-don. Thou shalt here-af-ter o'er E-gypt with
Amneris.
(Ven-ga la schia-va, ven-ga a ra-
(Now let you bond-maid, now let her
es-sa re-gne-rai.
her hold con-joint sway.

Maestoso come prima.
pirmi l'amor mio se
rob me of my love she
l'o_sa!)
dare not!)
Glo_ria all' E_git_to, ad I_si_de, che il sa_cro suol di_
Glo_ry to E_gypt's sacred land, I_sis hath aye pro_
Slave-prisoners.
Glo_ria al clemente E_gi_zi_o che i nostri ceppi ha
Glo_ry to E_gypt's gra_cious land, She hath revenge re_
Priests.
People.
Glo_ria all' E_git_to, ad I_si_de, che il sacro suol di_
Glo_ry to E_gypt's sa_cred land, I_sis hath aye pro_
Maestoso come prima.
ff

Ramphis.
fen - de, s'in - trec-ci il lo - to al lau - ro, s'in - trec - ci il lo - to al
tect - ed, With lau-rel and with lo - tus, with lau - rel and with
sciol - to, che ci ri - do - na ai li - be-ri, che ci ri - do - na ai
ject - ed, And lib - er - ty hath grant - ed us, and lib - er - ty hath
sciol - to, che ci ri - do - na ai li - be - ri, che ci ri - do - na ai
ject - ed, And lib - er - ty hath grant - ed us, and lib - er - ty hath
fen - de, s'in - trec - ci il lo - to al lau - ro, s'in - trec - ci il lo - to al
tect - ed, With lau - rel and with lo - tus, with lau - rel and with
fen - de, s'in - trec - ci il lo - to al lau - ro, s'in - trec - ci il lo - to al
tect - ed, With lau - rel and with lo - tus, with lau - rel and with
fen - de, s'in - trec - ci il lo - to al lau - ro, s'in - trec - ci il lo - to al
tect - ed, With lau - rel and with lo - tus, with lau - rel and with

cantabile
In - ni le - via - mo ad
Praise be to I - sis,
lau - ro sul crin, sul crin del vin - ci - tor.
lo - tus en - twine Proud - ly the vic - tor's head.
li - be - ri sol - chi del pa - trio suol.
grant - ed us Once more our soil to tread.
li - be - ri sol - chi del pa - trio suol.
grant - ed us Once more our soil to tread.
cantabile
In - ni le - via - mo ad
Praise be to I - sis,
cantabile
In - ni le - via - mo ad
Praise be to I - sis,
pesante
lau - ro sul crin, sul crin del vin - ci - tor.
lo - tus en - twine, twine we the vic - tor's head.
pesante
lau - ro sul crin del vin - ci - tor.
lo - tus twine we the vic - tor's head.
pesante
lau - ro sul crin, sul crin del vin - ci - tor.
lo - tus en - twine, twine we the vic - tor's head.
pesante
p staccato

Ramphis.
Priests.
I - - si - de_ che il sa-cro suol di - fen - de! Preghiam che il_ fa-ti ar-
god - dess bland, Who hath our land pro-tect - ed, And pray that the fa-vors
ri - dano, preghiam che il fa - ti ar - ri - da - no_ fau -
granted us, and pray the fa - vors_ grant-ed us_ Ev -
ff

Aïda.
(Qual spe - - me o-mai più re - sta - mi? A-
(A - las! to me what hope is left? He
Amneris.
(Dal - l'in-at-te-so
(Al - most of ev-'ry
Radamès.
(D'av-ver - - so Nu-me il fol - go - re sui
(Now heav- - en's bolt the clouds has cleft, Up-
Ramphis.
- stial-la pa-tria o-gnor.
- er_ be o'er us_ shed.
The King.
Glo-ria
Glo-ry
Priests.
- stial-la pa-tria o-gnor.
- er_ be o'er us_ shed.
- stial-la pa-tria o-gnor.
- er_ be o'er us_ shed.
People.
Glo-ria
Glo-ry
Glo-ria
Glo-ry
mf

lui la glo-ria, il tro - no - a me lo -
wed, a throne as-cend - ing I left my
giu - bi-lo i - nebbri-a-ta io so - no;
sense bereft, By joy my hopes transcending,
ca - - po mio di-scen - de ah no! d'E-gitto il
on my head descend - ing Ah! no all E-gypt's
Pre - ghiam che i fa - ti,
Pray that the fa - vors,
ad I - si-de!
to I - sis bland!
ad I - si-de!
to I - sis bland!
ad I - si-de!
to I - sis bland!
ad I - si-de!
to I - sis bland!

blio le la - - - - -
loss to mea - - - - -
tut - ti in un dì si com - - - pio - no i
scarce I the triumph can mea - - - sure Now
so - glio non val,
trea - sure Weighs not,
pre - ghiam che i fa - ti ar - ri - da - no
Pray that the fa - vors grant - ed us
glo - ria!
glo - ry!
glo - ria!
glo - ry!
glo - ria!
glo - ry!
glo - ria!
glo - ry!

cri-me d'un di - - - spe-ra - to a -
sure, To mourn a hope - less
so - - gni del mio cor, i so-gni del mi - o
crown - ing all my love, now crown-ing all my
non val, non val d'Ai - da il
weighs not, weighs not Ai - da's
fau - - sti al - la pa - tria o - gnor, fausti alla pa - tria o - - -
Ev - - er be o'er us shed, ev - er be o'er us
glo - - - -
glo - - - -
glo - - - -
glo - - - -
glo - - - -
glo - - - -

Molto più mosso, quasi tempo doppio.
mor.
love.
cor.
love.
cor.
love.
Amonasro.
(to Aïda)
Fa cor: de - la tua pa - tria i lie - ti e - ven - tia -
Take heart: there yet some hope is left, Thy coun - try's fate a -
gnor.
shed.
ria!
ry!
ria!
ry!
ria!
ry!
Molto più mosso, quasi tempo doppio.
pp
spet - ta; per noi del - la ven - det - ta già pros - si - mo è l'al -
mend - ing; Soon shalt thou see with pleas - ure Re - venge light from a -
pp

A me l'o - bli - -
I left to mourn my
Tut-te in un dì si com-pio - no le gio -
Scarce can I mea - sure now the triumph, the tri -
Qual i - nat - te - - so fol - go - re! qual
Now heaven's bolt the cloud hath cleft! now
bor. Fa cor,
bove. Take heart,
In - - ni
Praise be
Glo-ria al-l'E - git- -to!
Glo - ry to E- -gypt!
Chorus of Priests.
In -
Praise
In- - ni
Praise be

o, a me l'o-blio, le la - cri - me, le la - cri-
loss, Mourn for my loss, to mourn my love, my hope - less
je del mi-o cor.
umph of all my love.
i - nat - te - so fol - go - re sul capo mio dis-cen -
heaven's bolt the cloud hath cleft, up- -on my head descend -
fa co - re, fa cor, fa
take heart a - gain, take heart a-
le - viam ad I - si - de,
to I - sis, the god - dess bland,
gloria, gloria, gloria,
glory, glory, glory,
TENORS.
ni le - viam, in - ni le -
be to her, to her be
BASSES.
le - viam ad I - si - de,
to I - sis, the god - dess bland,
Priests.
Gloria, gloria, gloria,
Glory, glory, glory,
Gloria, gloria, gloria,
Glory, glory, glory,
Gloria, gloria, gloria,
Glory, glory, glory,
Chorus of People.

Sostenuto come prima
p
me. Ah! qual spe- - me o-mai più
love. Ah! what hope, a - las, to
Ah!
Ah!
de! Ah! qual in- - at - te - so
ing! Ah! now heav- - en's bolt the
cor. Ah! fa cor,
gain. Ah! take heart,
In - ni le - via - mo ad
Praise be to I - sis,
gloria al-l'E - git - to! Glo - - ria, glo - ria al - l'E-git - to ad
glo - ry to E - gypt! Glo - - ry, glo - ry to E - gypt's
Prisoners. Slaves.
Glo - ria al clemen - te E -
Glo - ry to E - gypt's
Glo - ria al clemen - te E -
Glo - ry to E - gypt's
viam. In - ni le - via - mo ad
praise. Praise be to I - sis,
In - ni le - via - mo ad
Praise be to I - sis,
Ah! glo - ria al-l'Egit - to ad
Ah! glo - ry to E - gypt's
glo-ria al-l'E - git - to! Glo - ria, glo - ria al-l'Egit - to ad
glo - ry to E - gypt! Glo - ry, glo - ry to E - gypt's
glo-ria al-l'E - git - to! Glo - ria.
glo - ry to E - gypt! Glo - ry.
Sostenuto come prima. (♩=88.)
pp cresc. molto
ff
allarg.

re - sta - mi? a lui la glo-ria il
me is left? He wed, a throne as -
Dal - l'i-nat-te-so gau - dio
Al - most of ev - 'ry sense bereft,
fol - go - re sul ca - po mio di -
cloud hath cleft, Up - on my head des -
fa cor: la tua
take heart, yes, some
I - si - de, che il sa - cro suol di -
god - dess bland, Who hath our land pro -
I - si - de, che il sa - cro suol di -
god - dess bland, Who hath our land pro -
gi - zi - o che i nostri cep - pi ha
gra - cious land, Who hath revenge re -
gi - zi - o che i nostri cep - pi ha
gra - cious land, Who hath revenge re -
I - si - de, che il sa - cro suol di -
god - dess bland, Who hath our land pro -
I - si - de, che il sa - cro suol di -
god - dess bland, Who hath our land pro -
I - si - de, che il sa-cro suol di -
god - dess bland, Who hath our land pro -
I - si - de, che il sa-cro suol di -
god - dess bland, Who hath our land pro -
I - si - de,
god - dess bland,

tro - no a me l'o -
cend - ing I left, my
i - nebbri - a - ta jo so - no;
By joy all hope trans - cend - ing;
scen - de! ah no! d'E - git - to il
cend - ing! Ah no! all E - gypt's
pa - tria i lie - ti e - ven - ti a -
hope is left, Thy coun - try's fate a -
fen - de! pre - ghiam che i fa - ti ar -
tect - ed! Pray we the fa - vor
fen - de! s'in - trec - ci il lo - to al
tect - ed! With lau - rel and with
sciol - to, che ci ri - do - na ai
ject - ed, And lib - er - ty hath
sciol - to, che ci ri - do - na ai
ject - ed, And lib - er - ty hath
fen - de! pre - ghiam che i fa - ti ar -
tect - ed! Pray we the fa - vor
fen - de! pre - ghiam che i fa - ti ar -
tect - ed! Pray we the fa - vor
fen - de! s'in - trec - ci il lo - to al
tect - ed! With lau - rel and with
fen - de! s'in - trec - ci il lo - to al
tect - ed! With lau - rel and with

blio, le la - - -
loss to mea - -
tut - te in un dì - si com - - pio - no - le
scarce I the triumph can mea - - sure, Now
tro - - no non val
trea - - sure Weighs not,
spet - ta; per noi del - la ven -
mend - ing; Thou'lt soon behold with
ri - da - no, pre - ghiam che i fa - ti ar - ri - da -
grant - ed us, pray we the fa - vor grant - ed
lau - ro, s'in - trec - ci il lo - to al
lo - tus, with lau - rel and with
li - be - ri, che ci ri - do - na ai
grant - ed us, and lib - er - ty hath
li - be - ri, che ci ri - do - na ai
grant - ed us, and lib - er - ty hath
ri - da - no, pre - ghiam che i fa - ti ar - ri - da -
grant - ed us, pray we the fa - vor grant - ed
ri - da - no, pre - ghiam che i fa - ti ar - ri - da -
grant - ed us, pray we the fa - vor grant - ed
lau - ro, s'in - trec - ci il lo - to al
lo - tus, with lau - rel and with
lau - ro, s'in - trec - ci il lo - to al
lo - tus, with lau - rel and with

cri me d'un di - spe-ra - to a -
- sure, To mourn a hope - less
gio - je del mio cor, le gio - je del mio
crown - ing all my love, crown - ing all my
non val, non val d'A - ï - da il
weighs not, weighs not A - ï - da's
det - ta già pros-simo è l'al -
plea - sure Vengeance light from a -
no fau - sti al - la pa - tria,
us Ev - er, ev - er be o'er us,
lau - ro sul crin, sul crin del vin - ci -
lo - tus en - twine Proud - ly the vic - tor's
li - be - ri sol - chi del pa - trio
grant - ed us Once more our soil to
li - be - ri sol - chi del pa - trio
grant - ed us Once more our soil to
no fau - sti al - la pa - tria,
us Ev - er, ev - er be o'er us,
no fau - sti al - la pa - tria,
us Ev - er, ev - er be o'er us,
lau - ro sul crin, sul crin del vin - ci -
lo - tus en - twine, twine we the vic - tor's
lau - ro sul crin del vin - ci -
lo - tus twine we the vic - tor's
lau - ro sul crin, sul crin del vin - ci -
lo - tus en - twine, twine we the vic - tor's

Più mosso. (♩= 132.)
mor, a me l'o - bli - o, l'o - bli - o,
love, I left to measure, to measure
cor, tut - te del cor, tut - te
love, all, all my love, scarce can
cor, d'E - git - to il suol non va - le,
love, all E - gypt's wealth weighs not,
bor, per noi del - la,
bove, soon shalt thou, soon
in - ni le - via - mo ad I - si - de, che il sa - cro suol, che il sa - cro
Praise be to I - sis, god - dess bland, Who hath our soil, who hath our
tor, s'in - trec - ci il lo - to,
head, with lau - rel and lo - tus,
suol, che ci ri - do - na, ri - do - na,
tread, and hath our free - dom, our free - dom,
suol, che ci ri - do - na, ri - do - na,
tread, and hath our free - dom, our free - dom,
in - ni le - via - mo ad I - si - de, che il sa - cra suol, che il sa - cro
Praise be to I - sis, god - dess bland, Who hath our soil, who hath our
in - ni le - via - mo ad I - si - de, che il sa - cra suol, che il sa - cro
Praise be to I - sis, god - dess bland, Who hath our soil, who hath our
tor, s'in - trec - ci il lo - to al lau - ro,
head, with lau - rel, and with, with lau - rel,
tor, s'in - trec - ci il lo - to al lau - ro sul crin, sul crin del vin - ci -
head, with lau - rel and with lo - tus en - twine, en - twine the vic - tor's
tor, s'in - trec - ci il lo - to,
head, with lau - rel, with lo - tus,
Più mosso. (♩= 132.)
mf

sempre animando
le - la - cri -
all, all my
si com - pio -
I meas - ure
non va - le, non val d'A - i - da il
weighs not, weighs not A - i - da's
del - la ven - det - ta già pros - si - mo è l'al - bor, del - la ven -
shalt thou with plea - sure see vengeance from a - bove, soon thou'lt see
suol di - fen - de, pre - ghiam che i fa - ti ar - ri - da -
soil pro - tect - ed, pray we the fa - vor grant - ed
il lo - to al lau - ro sul crin del vin - ci - tor, il lo - to al
laurel and lo - tus en - twine the vic - tor's head, with lau - rel,
che ci ri - do - na ai li - be - ri sol - chi del
And hath our free - dom now grant - ed us once more our
che ci ri - do - na ai li - be - ri sol - chi del
And hath our free - dom now grant - ed us once more our
ff
suol di - fen - de, pre - ghiam che i fa - ti ar - ri - da -
soil pro - tect - ed, pray we the fa - vor grant - ed
ff
suol di - fen - de, pre - ghiam che i fa - ti ar - ri - da -
soil pro - tect - ed, pray we the fa - vor grant - ed
il lo - to al lau - ro, il lo - to al lau - ro sul
lau - rel and lo - tus, with lau - rel and lo - tus en -
tor, sul crin, s'in - trec - ci il lo - to al - lau - ro sul
head, en - twine with lau - rel and with lo - tus, en -
il lo - to al lau - ro sul crin del vin - ci - tor, il lo - to al
lau - rel and lo - tus en - twine the vic - tor's head, with lau - rel
8
sempre animando

me d'un di-spe-ra - to a-
lose, To mourn a hope - less
no le gio-je del mio
all the tri-umph of my
cor, ah no, non val d'A - i - da il
love, ah no, weighs not A - i - da's
det-ta già pros - si-mo è l'al-
vengeance light from, light from a-
no fau-sti al-la pa-tria, al-la pa - tria o-
us ev-er be o'er us, be o'er us
lau - ro sul crin del vin - ci-
lo - tus en-twine the vic - tor's
pa-tri-o suol, del pa - trio
na-tive soil to tread, our soil to
pa-tri-o suol, del pa - trio
na-tive soil to tread, our soil to
no fau-sti al-la pa-tria, al - la pa - tria o-
us ev-er be o'er us, be o'er us
no fau-sti al-la pa-tria, al - la pa - tria o-
us ev-er be o'er us, be o'er us
crin del vin-ci-tor, del vin - ci-
twine the vic-tor's head, the vic - tor's
crin del vin-ci-tor, del vin - ci-
twine the vic-tor's head, the vic - tor's
lau - ro sul crin del vin - ci-
lo - tus en-twine the vic - tor's
ff

mor, a me l'o -
love, I left to
cor, le
love, the
cor, d'E - git - to il
love, all E - gypt's
bor, per noi, per noi del - la ven - det - ta già
bove, yes, soon, yes, soon shalt thou see ven - geance light
gnor, preghiam, pre - ghiam che i fa - ti ar - ri - da - no fau -
shed, we pray, we pray the fa - vor grant - ed us ev -
tor, s'in - trec - ci il lo - to, il lo - to al lau - ro sul
head, with lau - rel and with lo - tus, lo - tus en -
suol, del
tread, our
suol, glo - ria al cle - men - te E - gi - zio, glo - ria
tread, glo - ry to E - gypt, to E - gypt, glo - ry,
gnor, pre - ghiam, pre - ghiam che i fa - ti ar - ri - da - no fau -
shed, we pray, we pray the fa - vor grant - ed us ev -
gnor, pre - ghiam, pre - ghiam che i fa - ti ar - ri - da - no fau -
shed, we pray, we pray the fa - vor grant - ed us ev -
tor, del
head, the
tor, sul crin del
head, twine we the
tor, s'in - trec - ci il lo - to, il lo - to al lau - ro sul
head, with lau - rel and with lo - tus, lo - tus en -

bli - - - - - o,
mea - - - - - sure
gio - - - - - je
tri - - - - - umph
so - - - - - glio
trea - - - - - sure
pros - si - mo è l'al - bor, per noi, per noi del - la ven -
from a - bove, a - bove, yes, soon, yes, soon shalt thou see
sti al - la pa - tria o - gnor, pre - ghiam, pre - ghiam che i fa - ti ar -
ver, be o'er us shed, pray we, pray we, the fa - vor
crin del vin - ci - tor, s'in - tre - ci il lo - to il lo - to al
twine the vic - tor's head, with lau - rel and with lo - tus
pa - - trio suol,
soil to tread,
glo - - - - ria, glo - ria al cle - men - te E -
glo - - - - ry, glo - ry to E - gypt to
sti al - la pa - tria o - gnor, pre - ghiam, pre - ghiam che i fa - ti ar -
er be o'er us shed, pray we, yes, pray the fa - vor
sti al - la pa - tria o - gnor, pre - ghiam, pre - ghiam che i fa - ti ar -
er be o'er us shed, pray we, yes, pray the fa - vor
vin - - ci - tor,
vic - - tor's head,
vin - - ci - tor,
vic - - tor's head,
crin del vin - ci - tor, s'in - tre - ci il lo - to il lo - to al
twine the vic - tor's head, with lau - rel and with lo - tus

le la - cri - me d'un
all, all my loss, Mourn -
del mi - o cor, le
of all my love, the
non val d'A - i - da il cor, non
Weighs not A - i - da's love, weighs,
det - ta già pros - si - mo è l'al - bor, già
ven - geance light from, light from a - bove, light
ri - da - no fau - sti al - la pa - tria o gnor, fau -
grant - ed us Ev - er be o'er us shed, ev -
lau - ro sul crin del vin - ci - tor, sul
lo - tus En - twine the vic - tor's head, en -
del pa - trio suol, del
our soil to tread, our
gi - zio, glo - ria, glo - ria al
E - gypt, glo - ry, glo - ry be
ri - da - no fau - sti al - la pa - tria o - gnor, fau -
grant - ed us ev - er be o'er us shed, ev -
ri - da - no fau - sti al - la pa - tria o - gnor, fau -
grant - ed us ev - er be o'er us shed, ev -
del vin - ci - tor, sul
the vic - tor's head, twine
sul crin del vin - ci - tor, sul
twine we the vic - tor's head, twine
lau - ro sul crin del vin - ci - tor, sul
lo - tus en - twine the vic - tor's head, twine

di - - spe - - - ra - to a
ing my hope - less
gio - je del
tri - umph of my
val d'A - - i - da il
not A - - i - da's
pros - - - si - mo è l'al -
from light from a -
sti al - - la pa - tria o
er be o'er us
crin del vin - ci -
twine the vic - tor's
pa - trio, pa - trio
soil, our soil to
l'E gi - zio glo -
on E - gypt aye,
sti al - - la pa - tria o -
er be o'er us
sti al - - la pa - tria o -
er be o'er us
crin del vin - ci -
we the vic - tor's
crin del vin - ci -
we the vic - tor's

Tempo I.
mor.)
love.)
cor.)
love.)
cor.)
love.)
bor.
bove.
gnor.
shed.
tor.
head.
suol.
tread.
ria.
shed.
gnor.
shed.
gnor.
shed.
tor.
head.
tor.
head.
Tempo I. (♩= 100)
3

End of Act II.

Act III.

Introduction, Prayer-Chorus.

Romanza.

Aïda.

Shores of the Nile. – Granite rocks overgrown with palm-trees. On the summit of the rocks, a temple dedicated to Isis, half hidden in foliage. Night; stars and a bright moon.

Chorus (in the Temple).
Tutti.
TENOR.
O tu che sei d'O-si-ri-de madre immorta-le e spo-sa,
Oh, thou who to O-si-ris art moth-er and con-sort im-mor-tal,
BASS.
O tu che sei d'O-si-ri-de madre immorta-le e spo-sa,
Oh, thou who to O-si-ris art moth-er and con-sort im-mor-tal,
p
Ped.
Di-va che i ca-sti pal-pi-ti desti a gli u-ma-ni in cor;
God-dess that mak'st the hu-man heart in fond e-mo-tion move,
Di-va che i ca-sti pal-pi-ti desti a gli u-ma-ni in cor;
God-dess that mak'st the hu-man heart in fond e-mo-tion move,
High Priestess.
ben legato
f
ff
Soc-cor-ri, soc-cor-ri a noi,
Aid, aid us thy por-tal who seek,
Soc-cor-ri a noi, pie-
Aid us who seek thy
Soc-cor-ri a noi, pie-
Aid us who seek thy

(From a boat which approaches the shore descend Amneris and Ramphis, followed by some women closely veiled. Guards.)

pp
I-si-de leg-ge de' mor - ta - li nel co-re; o-gni mi-ste-ro
To I-sis are the hearts of mor-tals... o-pen; In hu-man hearts what-
de-gli u-ma-ni a le-i no-to,
e'er is hid-den, full well she know-eth.
Amneris.
cantabile
Sì; io pre-ghe-
Ay; and I will
pp
pp
rò che Ra-da-mès mi do-ni tut-to il suo cor, co-me il mio
pray that Ra-da-mès may give me tru-ly his heart, tru-ly as
cor a lui sa-cro è per sem-pre.
mine to him was ev-er de-vot-ed.
Ramphis.
An-diamo. Pre-ghe-rai fi-no al
Now en-ter. Thou shalt pray till the
p
ppp

(all enter the temple)
l'al-ba; io sa-rò te-co.
day-light; I shall be near thee.
Chorus: Priestesses.
Soc - - cor-ri, soc-cor-ri a noi,
Aid, aid us thy por-tal who seek,
Chorus.
portando la voce
Soc-
oh
TENOR.
Soc-cor-ri a noi, pie-to - sa, ma-dre d'immenso a-mor, soc-
Aid us who seek thy por - tal, parent of deathless love, oh
BASS.
Soc-cor-ri a noi, pie-to - sa, ma-dre d'immenso a-mor,
Aid us who seek thy por - tal, parent of deathless love,
p
p
ff
cor- - ri a noi, soc - cor - ri a noi.
aid us, oh aid us thy por-tal who seek.
morendo
ff
cor- - ri a noi, soc - cor - ri a noi.
aid us, oh aid us thy por-tal who seek.
morendo
ff
morendo

(Scena vuota.)
sotto voce
sotto voce
ppp
(Aïda enters cautiously, veiled.)
ppp
Aïda.
Recit.
(lungo silenzio.)
Qui Ra-da-mès ver-rà! Che vor-rà
He will ere long be here! What would he
Recit.
(idem.)
dir-mi? Io tre-mo! Ah! se tu
tell me? I trem-ble! Ah! if thou

vie-ni a re-car-mi, o cru-del, l'ul-ti-mo ad-di-o, del
com-est to bid me, harsh man, fare-well for ev-er, then
Ni-lo i cu-pi vor-ti-ci
Ni-lus, thy dark and rush-ing stream
mi da-ran tom-ba
shall soon o'er-whelm me;—
e pa-ce for-se e pa-ce for-se e o-bli-o.
peace shall I find there, peace and a long ob-liv-ion.
morendo
Andante mosso. (♩= 92.)
p legato

a piacere
Oh pa-tria mia, mai più, mai più ti ri-ve-
My na-tive land no more, no more shall I be-
col canto
drò!
hold!
mai più!
no more!
p
mai più ti ri-ve-drò!
no more shall I be-hold!
dim. dolcissimo
Lo stesso movimento. (♩. = 92.)
cantabile
O cieli az-zur-ri, o dol-ci au-re na-ti-
O sky of a-zure hue, breez-es soft blow-
pppp
sfumato
il do ♯.
ve, do-ve se-re-no il mio mat-tin bril-
ing, Whose smiling glanc-es saw my young life un-
16
24

13573

dolciss.
lo o ver - di
fold Fair ver - dant
col - - li o pro - fu - ma - te
hill - - sides, oh stream - lets gen - tly
poco cresc.
ri - - ve o pa - tria
flow - - ing Thee, oh my
mi - - a, mai più ti ri - ve -
coun - - try, no more shall I be -
lunga
dro! oh pa - tria mi - a, mai
hold! espress. thee, oh my coun - try, no
legato

più, ah! mai più, ma - i più ti ri-ve - drò! oh pa-tria mia, oh pa-tria
more, ah! no more, ah no more shall I be - hold! My na-tive land, my na-tive
pp
p
cresc.
f
pp
rall.
mi - - a, mai più ti ri-ve - drò!
land no more shall I be - hold!
ppp col canto
pp parlante
mai più!
No more!
parlato
Cantabile.
no no mai più, mai più! O fre-sche
no no no more, no more! Yes, fra-grant
ten.
ppp

dolciss.
sfumate
val - li, o que - to a - sil be - a - - to che un di pro -
val - leys, your shel - ter - ing bow - - ers Once 'twas my
mes - so dal - l'a - mor mi fu
dream should love's a - bode hang o'er
dol.
Or che d'a -
Per - ish'd those
mo - re il so - gno è di - le - gua - to o pa - tria
dreams now like win - ter - blighted flow - ers, Land of my
poco più f
mi - a, non ti ve - drò mai più!
fa - thers, ne'er shall I see thee more!
espr.
legato
pp
oh pa - tria mi - a, non ti ve - drò mai più! no, mai
land of my fa - thers, ne'er shall I see thee more! no, no

dol.
senza affrett.
più non ti ve-drò, non ti ve-drò mai più!
more, ne'er shall I see, ne'er shall I see thee more!
pp
col canto
pp
legato
pp con forza
dim.
allarg. ppp
oh patria mia, mai più ti ri-ve-
Oh native land, I ne'er shall see thee
pp
smorz.
drò!
more!
allarg.
ppp

Duet.

Aïda and Amonasro.

declamato.
va - le razza in - fa - me, ab - bor - ri - ta ea noi fa -
ri - val race ac - curs - ed, race de - test - ed, to us aye
Aïda.
fiero.
E in suo po - te - re io sto! Io d'A - mo - na - sro fi - glia!
And I am in her grasp! I, A - mo - na - sro's daugh - ter!
ta - le!
fa - tal!
In po - ter di
In her pow - er
lei! No! se lo bra - mi, la pos - sen - te ri - val tu vin - ce - ra - i, e
thou! No! if thou wish - est, thy all - pow - er - ful ri - val thou shall van - quish, thy
pp
ff
morendo.
pa - tria, e tro - no, ea - mor, tut - to tu a - vra - i.
coun - try, thy scep - tre, thy love, shall all be thine.
p
p
pp

Allegro giusto. (♩=100)
cantabile, dolciss.
Ri - ve - drai le fo - re-ste im-bal - sa - ma - te, le fre-sche
Once a - gain shalt thou on our balm - y for - ests, our ver-dant
dolciss.
Aïda.
(with transport.)
val - li, i no-stri tem-pli d'ôr!... Ri - ve - drò le fo - re-ste im-bal - sa -
val - leys, our gold-en tem-ples gaze!... Once a - gain shall I on our balm - y
dolciss.
ma - te! le fre-sche val - li, i no-stri tem-pli d'ôr!...
for - ests, our ver-dant val - leys, our gold-en tem-ples gaze!...
Amonasro.
Spo-sa fe -
The hap-py
li - ce a lui che a-ma-sti tan - to, tri - pu-dii im-men - si i - vi po-trai gio -
bride of thy heart's dear-est trea - sure, de-light un-bound - ed there shalt thou en -
col canto.

(with transport.)
Aida.
ir.__ Un gior-no so - lo di sì dol-ce in-can-to__ u-n' o-ra, u-
joy.__ One day a - lone of such en-chant-ing plea-sure__ nay, but an
cresc.
Amonasro.
cupo.
n'o - ra di__ tal__ gio-ia, e poi mo-rir! e poi mo-rir! Pur ram-
hour__ of bliss so__ sweet, then let me die! then let me die! Yet re-
men - ti che a noi l'E - gi-zio im-mi - te, le ca - se, i tem-pii e l'a-re pro-fa-
call how E-gyp-tian hordes de-scend - ed On our homes, our tem-ples, our al-tars dar'd pro-
pp
nò__ tras-se in cep-pi le ver-gi-ni ra-pi - te__ ma-dri__
fane__ Cast in bonds sis-ters, daugh-ters un - de - fend - ed, Moth-ers__
p

ten
Aïda. appassionato.
vec - chi fan - ciul - li ei tru - ci - dò. Ah! ben ram -
gray - beards, and help - less chil - dren slain. Too well re -
col canto.
ff
dolcissimo.
men - to quegl' in - fau - sti gior - ni! ram - men - to i
mem - ber'd are those days of mourn - ing! All the keen
Cantabile.
pp
lut - ti che il mio cor sof - fri! Deh!
an - guish my poor heart that pierc'd! Gods!
dolcissimo.
fa - te, o Nu - mi, che per
grant in mer - cy, peace once

noi ri - tor - ni, che per
more re - turn - ing, peace once
Amonasro.
Ram-men - ta!
Re-mem - ber!
noi ri - tor - ni l'al-ba in-vo-ca-ta de' se-re-ni
more re - turn - ing, Once more the dawn soon of glad days may
Non fia che tar -
Lose not a mo -
di.
burst.
parlante
di. In ar-mi o-ra si de-sta il po-pol
ment. Our peo-ple arm'd are pant-ing For the
Poco più animato. (♩= 116)
fz pp

nos-tro; tut-to è pron-to già Vit-to-ria a-
sig-nal when to strike the blow Suc-cess is
vrem, So-lo a sa-per mi re-sta qual sen-
sure, On-ly one thing is want-ing: That we
Aïda.
Chi sco-prir-lo po-
Who that path will dis-
tier il ne-mi-co se-gui-rà.
know by what path will march the foe.
tri-a? chi mai?
cov-er? canst tell?
Tu stes-sa!
Thy-self will!

I-o!
I!
sotto voce.
Ra-da-mès so che qui at-tendi.
Ra-da-mès knows thou art wait-ing.
col canto.
ppp
ppp
Amonasro.
Ei t'a-ma
He loves thee,
ei con-du-ce gli E-gi-zii
he commands the E-gy tians
Aïda.
Or-ro- - -re! Che mi con-si-gli
O hor- - -ror! What wilt thou that I
In-ten-di?
Dost hear me?
ff
tu?
do?
No! no! giam-mai!
No! nev-er-more!
Su
Up,
ff

Allegro. (♩.= 96)
(with savage fury)
ff
mf
dun - - que! sor - get - te e - gi - zie co -
E - - - gypt! fierce na - tion Our cit - ies de -
or - ti! col fuo - co strug - ge - te le no - stre cit - tà.
vot - ing To flames, and de - not - ing With ru - ins your path.
tutta forza.
Spar - ge - - - - te il ter -
Spread wide de - vas -
ro - re, le stragi, le mor - ti al vos - tro fu - ro - re più fre - no non
ta - tion, Your fu - ry un - brid - le. Re - sistance is i - dle, Give rein to your

Aïda.
Ah! pa-dre! pa-dre! Pie-tà! pie-
Ah! Fa-ther! Fa-ther! (repulsing her) Nay hold! nay
v'ha. Mia fi-glia ti chiami!
wrath. Dost call thee my daughter?
mf
ff
tà! pie-tà!
hold! have mer - cy!
mezza voce
Flut-ti di san - gue scor - ro - no
Tor-rents of blood shall crim - son flow,
ff
dim.
sul-le cit-tà dei vin - ti.....
Grim-ly the foe stands gloat - ing.....
Ve-di? dai ne - gri
Seest thou? from dark - ling
vor - ti - ci
gulfs be - low
si le-va-no gli e-stin - ti
Shades of the dead up-float - ing!

sotto voce e cupo
ti ad-di-tan es - si e gri - da-no: per te la pa-tria
Cry-ing, as thee in scorn they show: "Thy coun-try thou hast
ppp
col canto
cupo
ppp
Aïda.
Pie-tà! pie-tà! pa-dre, pie - tà!
Nay hold! ah hold! have mer-cy, pray!
muor!
slain"!
ppp
sotto voce.
U-na lar-va or-ri-bi-le fra l'om-bre a noi s'af-fac-cia
One a-mong those phan-toms dark, E'en now it stands be-fore thee
sempre pp
ppp

Aïda
senza suono.
Ah!
Ah!
Amonasro.
tre-ma! le scar-ne brac-cia sul ca-po tuo le-vò
Trem-ble! now stretching o'er thee, Its bo-ny hand I mark
Padre! No! Ah!
Fa-ther! No! Ah!
Tua madre ell' è rav-vi-sa-la ti ma-le-
Thy mother's hands see there a-gain stretch'd out to
poco cresc.
(with the utmost terror.)
Ah! no! Ah! no! pa-dre, pie-tà! pie-tà! pie-
Ah! no! ah! no! my fa-ther, spare! ah spare! ah
di-ce.
curse thee.
ff

tà! pie-tà! pie - tà!
spare! ah spare thy child!
(repulsing her)
Non sei mia
Thou'rt not my
ff
fi - glia!
daugh-ter!
Dei Fa - ra - o - ni tu sei la
No, of the Pha - roahs thou art a
Aïda.
(uttering a cry.)
Ah!
Ah!
schiava!
bond-maid!
pie-
oh
fff
un poco allarg.
p
tà!
spare!
pie - tà! pie -
oh spare thy
ppp

Andante assai sostenuto. (♩ = 76)
(dragging herself to her father's feet.)
tà!
child!
ppp con espress.
pp con espress.
molto sotto voce e cupo
Pa-dre! a co-sto-ro schiava non
Fa-ther! no, their slave am I no
so-no Non ma-le-dir-mi non im-pre-
long-er Ah, with thy curse do not ap-

car - mi_ an - cor tua
pal me; Still thine own
fi - glia po - trai chia -
daugh - ter thou may - est
mar - - mi_ del - la mia
call me, Ne'er shall my
pa - tria, del - la mia pa - tria_ de - gna sa-
coun - try, ne'er shall my coun - try_ her child dis-

rò.
dain.
Amonasro.
Pen - sa che un po - - po -
Think that thy race, down -
pp
lo vin - to, stra - zia - - to
tram - pled by the con - - q'ror,
per te sol - tan - to, per te sol -
thro' thee a - lone, ay, thro' thee a -
3
Aïda.
tan - to ri - sor - ger può
lone can their free - dom gain.
Oh pa - tria! oh
Oh then my
cresc. poco a poco

pa - tria quan - to mi co - - - - sti! O
coun - try has prov'd the stron - - - - - ger, my
morendo
pa - tri - a! quan - to mi co - - - -
coun - try's cause than love is stron - -
ppppp
morendo
sti!
ger!
Amonasro.
(conceals himself among the palms)
Coraggio! ei giunge là tut - to u - drò.
Have courage! he comes there I'll remain.
dim. ed allarg. un poco

Duet.

Aïda and Radamès.

Scene.—Finale III.

marc.
Te ỉ ri - ti at - ten - dono d'un al - tro a - mor. D'Amne - ris
Thou to an - oth - er must thy hand re - sign. The Prin - cess
gui - da.
meet thee.
sposo.
weds thee!
accel.
Che par - li mai? Te so - la, A - i - da, te deg-gio a -
What say - est thou? Thee on - ly, A - i - da, e'er can I
string.
sempre staccato, accel.
D'u - no sper.
Invoke not
mar. Gli Dei m'a - scol - ta - no tu mia sa - ra - i
love. Be wit - ness, heav - en, thou art not for - sak - en
f al tempo I.

declamato
Aïda.
giu - ro non ti mac - chiar! Pro - de t'a - mai, non t'a - me - rei sper -
false - ly the gods a - bove! True, thou wert lov'd; let not un - truth de -
string.
giu - ro! E co - me spe - ri sot -
grade thee! And how then hop'st thou to
Radamès.
Del l'a - mor mi - o du - bi - ti, A - i - da?
Can of my love no more I per - suade thee?
Aïda.
poco a poco string.
trar - ti d'Am - ne - ris ai vez - zi, del Re al vo - ler, del tuo po - po - lo ai
baf - fle the love of the Princess, the King's high com - mand, the de - sire of the
p poco cresc.
vo - ti, dei Sa - cer - do - ti al - l'i - ra?
peo - ple, the cer - tain wrath of the priest - hood?
ff

Radamès.
Tempo I.
O - di-mi, A - i - da.
Hear me, A - i - da.
Nel fie - ro a -
Once more of
leggerissimo e stacc.
ne - li - to di nuo - va guer - ra il suo - lo E -
dead - ly strife with hope un - fad - ing the E - thiop
ti - o - pe si ri - de - stò...
has a - gain light - ed the brand...
I tuoi già in -
Al - read - y
va - do - no la no - stra ter - ra, io de - gli E -
they our bor - ders have in - vad - ed; All E - gypt's
gi - zii du - ce sa - rò.
ar - mies I shall com - mand.
Fra il suon, fra i
While shouts of

plau - si del - la vit - to - ria, al Re mi
tri - umph greet me vic - to - rious, To our kind
pro - stro, gli sve-lo il cor, Sa - rai tu il ser - to del - la mia
mon - arch my love dis - clos - ing, I thee will claim as my guerdon
m.s.
glo - ria, vi - vrem be - a - ti d'e - ter - no a - mo - re. Sa - rai tu il
glo - rious, With thee live ev - er in love re - pos - ing, I thee will
dim.
dol.
ser - to del - la mia glo - ria, vi - vrem be - a - ti d'e - ter - no a -
claim as glo - ri - ous guer - don, With thee live ev - er in love's re -
p

Aïda.
Nè d'Am-ne-ris pa-ven-ti il
Nay, but dost thou not fear then Am-
mor.
pose.
Più animato. (♩ = 144.)
p
vin-di-ce fu-ror? la sua ven-
ne-ris' fell re-venge? Her dreadful
det-ta, co-me fol-gor tre-men-da cadrà su me, sul padre mi-o, su
vengeance, like the lightning of heav-en on me will fall, up-on my father, my
f
tut-ti. In-van! tu nol po-tre-sti.—
na-tion. In vain wouldst thou at-tempt it.—
Radamès.
Io vi di-fen-do!
I will de-fend thee!
pp

Pur_ se tu
Yet_ if thou
m'a - mi_ an - cor s'a - pre u - na
lov'st me_ there still of - fers a
via di-scam - po a noi_ Fug-gir_
path for our es - cape_ To flee!
Radamès.
Qua - le? Fug-
Name it! To
ff
gi - re!
flee hence?
ff
Andantino. (♩= 84.)
Aïda.
sotto voce parlante
Fug -
Ah,
p con espress.
(with impulsive warmth.)
giam gli ar - do - ri i - no - spi - ti di que - ste lan - de ji -
flee from where these burn - ing skies Are all be - neath them

morendo
gnu - de; u - na no - vel - la pa - tri - a al
blight - ing; Toward re - gions new we'll turn our eyes, Our
Lo stesso movimento.
doleiss.
no - stro a - mor si schiu - de... Là - tra... fo - re - ste ver - gi - ni,
faith - ful love in - vit - ing... There, where the vir - gin for - ests rise,
m.s.
estremamente p
di fio - ri pro - fu - ma - te, in e - sta - si be -
'Mid fra - grance soft - ly steal - ing, Our lov - ing bliss con -
estremamente p
ppp
a - - te la ter - ra scor - de - rem, in e -
ceal - - ing, The world we'll quite for - get, 'mid lov -
- sta - si, in e - - sta - si la
- ing bliss, 'mid lov - - ing bliss the

dolciss.
senza affrett.
ter - - ra scor - de - rem.
world we'll quite for - get.
Radamès.
Sovra u - na ter - ra e -
To dis - tant countries
dolciss.
senza affrett.
con slancio
stra-nia te - co fug - gir do - vrei! ab - ban - do - nar la
rang-ing, With thee thou bid'st me fly! For oth - er lands ex -
dolciss.
pa - tria, la - re de' no - stri Dei! il suol dov' io rac -
chang - ing All 'neath my na - tive sky! The land these arms have
dolciss.
pp
col - si di glo - ria i pri - mi al - lo - ri, il ciel de' no - stri a -
guard - ed, That first fame's crown a - ward - ed, Where first I thee re -

Aïda.
dolce
Là tra foreste
There, where the virgin
mo-ri co-me scor-dar po-trem?
gard-ed, How can I e'er for-get?
pp
m.s.
pp
ver-gi-ni, di fio-ri pro-fu-ma-te, in
for-ests rise, 'Mid fra-grance soft-ly steal-ing, Our
Il ciel de' no-stri a-mo-ri co-me scor-dar po-
Where first I thee re-gard-ed, How can I e'er for-
ppp
m.s.
pp
estremamente p
e-sta-si be-a-te la ter-ra scor-de-
lov-ing bliss con-ceal-ing, The world we'll quite for-
trem? co-me scor-dar?
get? Can I for-get?
estremamente p
pp dolciss.

pp
rem, in e - - sta - si, in e - -
get, 'mid lov - - ing bliss, 'mid lov - -
pp
co - me scor - dar po - trem il ciel de' no - stri a - mor?
how can I e'er for - get where I be - held thee first?
dolciss.
- sta - si la ter - - - ra scor - de -
- ing bliss the world we'll quite for -
dolciss.
rem.
get. con forza
Sotto il mio ciel, più
Beneath our skies more
il ciel de' no - stri a - mo - ri co - me scor - dar po - trem?
where first I thee re - gard - ed, how can I e'er for - get?

li-be-ro l'a-mor ne fia con-ces-so; i-vi nel tempio j-stes-so gli stessi Numi a-
freely to our hearts will love be yield-ed; The gods thy youth that shielded, will not our love for-
pp
vrem, i-vi nel tempio j-stes-so gli stes-si Numi a-vrem, i-vi nel tempio j-
get, The gods thy youth that shield-ed will not our love for-get, The gods thy youth that
Radamès.
Abban-do-nar la pa-tria, l'a-re de' nostri Dei! il ciel de' nostri a-
For oth-er lands ex-changing All neath my na-tive sky! Where thee I first re-
ppp
morendo
dolce
stes-so gli stes-si Nu-mi a-vrem; fuggiam, fug-giam!
shielded will not our love for-get; ah, let us fly!
mo-ri co-me scor-dar po-trem? A-
garded, How can I e'er for-get? A-
pp

Allegro vivo.
Tu non m'a-mi!... Va! Va!
Me thou lov'st not! Go! Go!
(hesitating.)
i-da! Non t'a-mo? Mor-tal giammai nè
i-da! Not love thee? Ne'er yet in mortal
Allegro vivo.
Va! va!
Go! go!
di-o ar-se d'a-mor al par del mio pos-sen-te!
bo-som love's flame did burn with ar-dor so de-vour-ing!
ppp
t'at-tende al-l'a-ra Am-neris,... Giammai, di-ces-ti? Al-
yon waits for thee Am-neris! In vain, thou sayest? Then
No! giam-mai!
All in vain!
cresc.

ff
lor... piombi la scu-re su me, sul pa-dre mi - - - - - -
fall... the axe up - on me, and on my wretched fa - - - - - -
f
ff
Allegro assai vivo.
o.
ther.
(With impassioned resolution.)
Radamès.
ppp
Ah no! fug-gia-mo! Sì: fug - giam da que-ste mu-ra, al... de -
Ah no! we'll fly, then! Yes, we'll fly these walls now hat-ed, In... the
Allegro assai vivo. (𝅗𝅥 = 100.)
p cresc.
pp
pp
-ser-to insiem fug - gia-mo; qui sol re-gna la sven-tu-ra, là... si
des-ert hide our treasure, Here the land to love seems fat-ed, There all...
p
pp
schiude un ciel d'a - mor. I de - ser-ti in-ter-mi-na-ti a noi...
seems to smile on me. Boundless deserts no thought can measure, Where our...

poco stent.
ta-la-mo sa - ran-no, su noi gli a-stri bril-le - ran - no di più
bridal couch soon spreading, Star - ry skies, their lus-tre shedding, Be our
col canto
in tempo
Aïda.
Nel-la ter-ra av-ven - tu - ra - ta de' miei
In my na - tive land where lav - ish For - tune
ppp
lim - pi-do ful - gor.
lu - cid can-o - py.
in tempo
p cresc.
pp
pa-dri, il ciel ne at - ten-de; i - vi l'aura è imbal - sa-ma-ta, i - vi il
smiles, a heav'n a - waits thee, Balm - y airs the sense that ravish, Stray thro'
pp
suolo è a-ro-mi e fior. Fre-sche val-li e ver-di pra-ti a noi
ver-dant mead and grove. 'Mid the valleys where nature greets thee, We our

poco stent.
ta - - lamo sa - ran - no, su noi gli a - stri bril - le - ran - no di più
bridal couch soon spreading, Star - ry skies, their lus - tre shedding, Be our
col canto
molto riten.
lim - pi - do ful - gor. Vie - ni me - - - co, insiem fug -
lu - cid can - o - py. Fol - low me, to - geth - er
Radamès.
Vie - ni me - - - co, insiem fug -
Fol - low me, to - geth - er
f molto riten.
gia - mo que - sta ter - - - ra di do - lor, Vie - ni
fly - ing, Where all love doth still a - bide; Thou art
gia - mo que - sta ter - - - ra di do - lor, Vie - ni
fly - ing, Where all love doth still a - bide; Thou art

me - co_ t'a - mo, t'a - mo! a_noi du - ce fia l'a - mor, fia l'a -
lov'd with love un - dy-ing! Come,and love our steps shall guide, love shall
me - co_ t'a - mo, t'a - mo! a_noi du - ce fia l'a - mor, fia l'a -
lov'd with love un - dy-ing! Come,and love our steps shall guide, love shall
(they are hasting away, when suddenly Aïda pauses.)
mor. Ma, dimmi: per qual via e - vi - te -
guide. But, tell me: by what path shall we a -
mor.
guide.
f
pp
rem le schiere de-gli ar - ma - ti?
void a-light-ing on the sol-diers?
Il sen-tier scel - to dai no-stri a piom-bar sul ne -
By the path that we have cho-sen to fall on the

E quel sen - tier?
Say, which is that?
mi-co fia de-ser-to fi-no a do-ma-ni.
Ethiops,'twill be free un-til to-morrow.
Le go-le di
The gorg-es of
Radamès.
Ná-pa-ta.
Ná-pa-ta.
Amonasro.
Di Ná-pa-ta le go-le! i - vi sa-ran-no i
Of Ná-pa-ta the gorg-es! There will I post my
f
Oh! chi ci a-scol - ta?
Who has o'erheard us?
miei.
D'A-i-da il pa-dre e de-gli E-tio-pi il Re!
men!
A-i-da's fa-ther, E-thi-o-pia's King!
ff

Radamès. (overcome with surprise.)
(♩=120)
Tu! Amonasro! tu! il
Thou! Amonasro! thou! the
pp col canto
ff
pp
Re? Nu-mi! che dis-si? No non è
King? Heav-en! what say'st thou? No! it is
ff
ppp
stacc.
ver, non è ver, non è ver, no, no, no, non è
false, it is false, it is false, no, no, no, it is
portare
(tronca)
pausa
ver, no! so-gno de-li-rio è
false! no! sure-ly this can be but
f
ppp

Aïda.
Ah no! ti cal - ma, a - scol - ta - mi,
Ah no! be calm, and list to me,
Radamès.
que - sto!...
dream-ing!
Amonasro.
A te l'a - mor d'A -
In her fond love con -
all' a - mor mio t'af - fi - da.
Trust love, thy foot - step guiding.
straziante
Io son di - so - no -
My name for ev - er
i - da
fid - ing
un so - glio in - nal - ze - rà.
A throne thy prize shall be.
Radamès.
ra - to! io son di so - no - ra - to! per
brand - ed: my name for ev - er brand - ed! for

Aïda.
Radamès.
Amonasro.
Ti cal - ma!
Ah, calm thee!
te tra - dii la pa - tria! tra - dii la pa - tri - a!
thee I've play'd the trai - tor! the trai - tor I have play'd!
No: tu non sei col -
No: blame can never
pe - vo - le, non sei col - pe - vo - le: e - ra vo - ler, e - ra vo - ler del
fall on thee, no blame can fall on thee: it was by fate, it was by fate com -
ten.
col canto
Io
My
fa - to!
mand - ed.
son di - so - no - ra - to! io son di - so - no -
name for ev - er brand - ed! my name for ev - er
Ah no!
Ah no!
No!
No!
pp
mf

13573

Ah no!
Ah no!
ra - to! per te tra - dii la pa - tria! per
brand - ed! for thee I play'd the trai - tor! for
No! no: tu non
No! no: blame can
m.d.
m.s. cresc. assai
ti cal - - - - ma.
ah, calm thee.
te tra - dii la pa - tri - a!
thee the trai - tor I have play'd!
sei, non sei col - pe - vo - le. Vien: ol - tre il Nil ne at -
nev - er, nev - er fall on thee. Come, where be - yond the
in tempo
col canto
pp e staccato

ten - do - no i pro - di a noi de - vo - ti, là del tuo
Nile arrayed, War - ri - ors brave are wait - ing; There love thy
pp
pp
cor, del tuo co - re i vo - ti co -
wish, love each fond wish sat - ing, Thou
Amneris.
(from the temple.)
Tra - di -
Traitor
(dragging Radamès.)
ro - ne - rà l'a - mor. Vie - ni, vie - ni, vie - ni.
shalt be hap - py made. Come then, come then, come then.
p

Più presto.
Amneris.
tor!
vile!
Aïda.
La mia ri - val!
My ri-val here!
Amonasro.
L'o-pra
Dost thou
Più presto.(♩ = 144.)
ff
Radamès.
Prestissimo.
(rushing between them)
Ar - re - sta, in -
De - sist, thou
Amonasro.
(advancing with dagger towards Amneris)
mia a strugger vie - ni!
come to mar my pro - jects!
Muori!
Die then!
Prestissimo.(𝅗𝅥 = 120.)
Radamès.
(to Aïda and Amonasro)
sa - no!
madman!
Presto! fug - gi - te!
Fly quick! de - lay not!
Amonasro.
Ramphis.
Oh rabbia!
Oh fu - ry!
Guardie, o - là!
Soldiers, ad - vance!

Amonasro. (dragging Aïda)
Vie - ni, o fig - lia.
Come then, my daughter.
Ramphis. (to the guards.)
L'in - se - gui - te!
Fol - low af - ter!
sempre ff
Radamès.
(to Ramphis)
Sa - cer - do - te, io re - sto a te.
Priest of I - sis, I yield to thee.
col canto
ff
ff

End of Act III.

Act IV.

Scene and Duet.

Amneris and Radamès.

SCENE I. A hall in the King's palace.
On the left, a large portal leading to the subterranean hall of justice. A passage on the right, leading to the prison of Radamès.

Amneris.
Recit.
L'abbor-ri-ta ri-va-le a me sfug-gi-a
She, my ri-val de-test-ed, has es-cap'd me
(Recitative.)
mf
Allegro moderato.
Dai sa-cer-
And from the
do-ti Ra-da-mès at-ten-de dei tra-di-tor la pe-na Tra-di-tor e-gli non
priest-hood Ra-da-mès a-waits the sen-tence on a traitor. Yet a trai-tor he is
pausa lunga
pp
Allegro agitato. (♩=144)
è
not.
Pur ri-ve-lò di
Tho' he disclos'd the
f

guerra l'al-to se-gre-to_ e-gli fug-gir vo-le-a_ con lei fug-
weighty se-crets of warfare, flight was his true in-tention, and flight with
gi-re_ Tra-di-to-ri tut-ti! a morte! a mor-
her, too. They are trai-tors all, then! deserving to per-
ff
ff
te!
ish!
Oh! che mai par-lo?
What am I say-ing?
con
Io
I
Sempre pianissimo.
(♩= 92.)
legato
passione
l'a-mo, io l'a-mo sem-pre_ Di-spe-ra-to, in-sa-no è que-st'a-
love him, still I love_him:_ Yes, in-sane and desp'rate is the

mor che la mia vi- -ta strug - ge.
love my wretched life de - stroy - ing.
lungo silenzio
Oh! s'ei po - tes - se a - mar - mi! Vor-rei sal - var - lo.__ E
Ah! could he on - ly love me! I fain would save him.__ Yet
pp
pp
risoluto
come? Si ten - ti! Guardie: Ra - da - mès qui
can I? One ef - fort! Soldiers: Ra - da - mès bring
ff
Andante sostenuto.
ven - ga.
hith - er.
mf
f

(Enter Radamès, led by guards)
Amneris.
dim.
pp
Già i sa-cer-do-ti a-
Now to the hall the
ppp
con passione
du-nan-si ar - bi-tri del tuo fa - to;
priests pro-ceed. Whose judg-ment thou art wait - ing;
lunga e dim.
pur dell' ac-cu-sa or-ri - bi - le scol-par - ti an-cor t'è
Yet there is hope from this foul deed Thy-self of dis-cul-
con agitazione
animando un poco
da - to: ti scol - pa, e la tua gra - zia
pat - ing; Once clear to gain thy par - don
con espress.
ppp animando un poco
pp
ten.

portando la voce
con espress.
io pre-ghe-rò dal tro-no, e nun-zia di per-
I at the throne's foot kneel-ing, For mer-cy dear ap-
do-no, e nun-zia di per-do-no, di vi-ta, a te sa-rò.
peal-ing, for mercy dear ap-peal-ing, Life will I ren-der thee.
Radamès.
Di
From
p
mie di-scolpe i giu-di-ci mai non u-dran l'ac-cen-to; di-
me my judg-es ne'er will hear One word of ex-cul-pa-tion; In
ppp
lunga morendo
ppp
animando
p
nan-zi ai Numi, agl'uo-mi-ni nè vil, nè reo mi sen-to. Prof-
sight of heaven I am clear, Nor fear its rep-ro-ba-tion. My

portando
fer - se il lab-bro in-cau - to fa-tal segreto, è ve - ro, ma
lips I kept no guard on, The se - cret I im-part - ed, But
ten.
p
pp
p
pu - ro il mio pen-sie - ro, ma pu-ro il mio pen - sie - ro e l'onor mio re-
guilt - less and pure-heart-ed, but guiltless and pure-heart - ed From stain my honor's
p
Amneris.
string. un poco
Sal-va-ti dun-que e scol-pa-ti. Tu mor-rai
Then save thy life, and clear thyself. Wouldst thou die?
stò. No. La vi-ta ab-
free. No! My life is
string. un poco
pp
bor - ro; d'o - gni gau - dio la fon - te i-na-ri-
hate - ful! Of all plea - sure for ev - er 'tis di-
cresc. e string.
ppp

di - ta, sva - ni - ta o - gni spe - ran - za, sol bra-mo di mo-
vest - ed, with - out hope's priceless trea - sure, 'tis bet-ter far to
rir.
die.
Amneris
Mo - ri - re!
Wouldst die, then?
Più animato.
Cantabile.
Ah! tu dei vi - ve - re!
Ah! thou for me shalt live!
Più animato. (♩= 84)
Sì, al-l'a - mor mio vi - vra - i; per te le an-go - scie or-
Live, of all my love as - sur - ed; The keen - est pangs that
ppp legato
accentate
ri - bi - li di mor - te io già pro - va - i; t'a-
death can give, For thee have I en - dur - ed! By

mai, sof-fer - si tan - to ve-glia - i le not-ti in
love condemn'd to lan - guish, Long vig - ils I've spent in
dolciss.
grandioso
pian - to e pa - tria, e tro - no, e
an - guish, my coun - try, my pow - er, my
f
tro - no, e vi - ta,
pow - er, ex - is - tence,
tut - to da - re - i, tut-to, tut - to da-rei per
all I'd sur - ren - der, I would all sur - ren - der for
Radamès.
Per
For

te.
thee.
es - sa an-ch'io la pa - - tria, per es - sa an-ch'io la
her I too my coun - - try, for her I too my
m.d.
m.s.
pa - - tria e l'o-nor mio, e l'o-nor
coun - - try, hon - - or and life, ay, life and
Amneris.
Poco più.
Di lei non più!
No more of her!
mi - o tra-di - a.
hon - or sur-ren-der'd!
L'in-fa-mia m'at-
Dis-hon-or a-
Poco più. (♩= 100)

ten - de e vuoi ch'io vi - - - - va?
waits me, Yet thou wilt save me?
ff
Tempo I.
string. a poco a poco
Mi - se-ro ap-pien mi fe - sti, A - i - da a me to -
Thou all my hope hast shak - en, A - i - da thou hast
animando un poco
p
glie - sti, spen - ta l'hai for - se e in do-no of-fri la vi-ta a
tak - en; Hap - ly thou hast slain her, And yet of-fer-est life to
f
ff
Amneris.
Io di sua mor-te o - ri - gi - ne! No! vi-ve A-
I, on her life lay guilt-y hands? No! She is
me?
me?
ff

Più mosso.
i - da! Nei di-spe-ra-ti a - ne - li-ti del-
liv - ing! When rout-ed fled the sav - age bands, To
Vi - - ve!
Liv - - ing!
Più mosso.(♩=120.)
ppp
for - - de fug-gi - ti - ve
fate war's chances giv - ing,
animando un poco
sol cad - de il
per - ish'd her
animando un poco
pa - dre.
fa - ther.
Sparve nè
Van-ish'd, nor
Radamès.
Ed el - la?
And she then?

più no-vel-la s'eb-be:
aught heard we then fur-ther.
Gli Dei l'ad-
The gods her
Radamès.
dolce
du - - ca - no sal-va al-le pa-trie mu - ra, ej-gno-ri
path guide then, Safe to her home re - turn - ing, guard her, too,
dolce
Amneris.
Recitative.
Ma, s'io ti sal-va,
But if I save thee,
Radamès.
la sven-tu-ra di chi per lei mor - rà!
e'er from learning That I for her sake die!
ppp con canto

giu - rami che più non la ve - drai: A lei ri-nun - zia per
wilt thou swear her sight e'er to re - sign? Swear to renounce her for
No! pos - so!
I can - not!
ppp
sempre e tu vi - vrai! Anco u-na volta: a
ev-er, life shall be thine! Once more thy answer: wilt
f
No! pos - so!
I can - not!
lei ri - nun-cia: Mo - rir vuoi dunque, in - sa - no?
thou re-nounce her? Life's thread wouldst thou then sev - er?
f
È va - no!
No, nev - er!
Pronto a mo-
I am pre-

Allegro agitato.
Chi ti sal - va, scia - gu -
From the fate now hang - ing
rir son già.
pared to die.
Allegro agitato.(♩= 144.)
ff
f
ra - to, dal - la sor - te che t'a - spetta? In fu -
o'er thee, Who will save thee, wretched be-ing? She whose
ro - re hai tu can - gia - to un a - mor ch'e-gual non
heart could once a - dore thee, Now is made thy mor - tal
ha. De' miei pian - ti la ven - det - ta or dal
foe. Heav - en, all my an - guish see-ing, Will a -
pp
f
pp

ciel si com - pi - - rà, de' miei pian - ti la ven -
venge this cru - el blow, Heav - en, all my an - guish
ff
det - ta or dal ciel, dal
see - ing, Will a - venge, a -
Poco più sostenuto.
ciel si com - pi - rà.
venge this cru - el blow.
Radamès.
È la mor - te un ben su -
Void of ter - ror death now ap -
Poco più sostenuto. (♩= 120)
pp

Ah! chi ti sal - va?
Ah! who will save thee?
pre - mo se per lei mo-rir m'è da - to; nel su -
pear - eth, Since I die for her I cher - ish; In the
cresc.
f
stentato
pp
bir lè - stremo fa - to gau - dii im - men - si il cor a -
hour when I per - ish, With de - light my heart will
cresc.
f
De' miei pian - ti la ven - det - ta or dal
Heav - en, all my an - guish see - ing, Will a -
vrà, gau - dii im -
glow, Then with de -
Tempo I.
f

ciel, ciel, dal ciel si com - pi -
venge, a - venge, a - venge this mor - tal
men - si il cor a -
light my heart will
Tempo doppio lo stesso movimento.
rà. De' miei pianti la ven - det - ta
blow. All my anguish, heav - en see - ing,
vrà; l'i - ra u - ma - na più non te - mo, te - mo sol la tua pie - tà;
glow; Wrath no more this bo - som feareth, Scorn for thee a - lone I know;
Tempo doppio lo stesso movimento.
or dal ciel si
Will a - venge this
l'i - ra u - ma - na più non te - mo, te - mo sol la
Wrath no more this bo - som feareth, Scorn for thee a -

(Amneris, overcome, sinks on a chair.)
com - pi - rà.
cru - el blow.
(Exit Radamès, attended by guards.)
tua pie - tà.
lone I know.
ff
1

Scene of the Judgment.
Amneris, Ramphis and Chorus.

(The Priests cross and enter the subterranean hall.)
mor-te è il lut-to e-ter-no del mio cor se-gna-sti!
doom'd him to death, and me to ev-er-last-ing sor-row!
(sees the Priests.)
f
Ec-co i fa-ta-li, gl'i-ne-so-ra-ti mi-ni-stri di mor-te.
Now yonder come, re-morse-less, re-lent-less, his mer-ci-less judg-es.
Oh! ch'io non veg-ga quel-le bian-che lar-ve!
Ah! let me not behold those white-rob'd phantoms!
(covers her face with her hands)
pp
È in po-ter di co-sto-ro io stes-sa lo get-tai! io stessa!
He is now in their power; I 'twas, his fate that seal'd! I on-ly!
pp

io stessa lo gettai! e in poter di co - storo io stes-sa lo get - tai!
I on - ly, I a - lone! He is now in their pow-er, I have seal'd his fate!
Lo stesso movimento.
Ramphis.
Chorus.
Spir - to del Nu - me so-vra noi di - scen - di!
Heav - en - ly Spir - it, in our hearts de - scend - ing,
ne av - vi - va al rag - gio del - l'e - ter - na lu - ce;
Kin - dle of right-eous-ness the flame e - ter - nal;

pel lab-bro no-stro tua giu-sti-zia ap-pren - - di.
Un-to our sentence truth and right-eous-ness lend - - ing.
pel lab-bro no-stro tua giu-sti-zia ap-pren - - di.
Un-to our sen-tence truth and right-eous-ness lend - - ing.
pel lab-bro no-stro tua giu-sti-zia ap-pren - - di.
Un-to our sen-tence truth and right-eous-ness lend - - ing.
Allegro.
Amneris.
Nu-mi, pie-tà del mio stra - zia - to
Pit-y, oh heav'n, this heart so sore - ly
Allegro. (♩ = 120.)
pp
co - re! Egli è in - no - cen-te, lo sal-va-te, o
wound - ed! His heart is guilt-less, save him pow'rs su -

Nu - mi! Di-spe - ra - to, tremendo è il mio do-lo - re!
per - nal! For my sorrow is despair - ing, deep, un-bound - ed!
(sees Radamès, and exclaims)
Oh! chi lo sal - va?
Ah! who will save him?
(Radamès crosses with guards, and enters the subterranean hall.)
Ramphis.
Spir - to del Nu - me so - vra noi di - scen - di!
Heav - en - ly Spir - it, in our heart descend - ing!
Spir - to del Nu - me so - vra noi di - scen - di!
Heav - en - ly Spir - it, in our heart de - scend - ing!
Spir - to del Nu - me so - vra noi di - scen - di!
Heav - en - ly Spir - it, in our heart de - scend - ing!
tutta forza
Amneris.
morendo
Oh! chi lo sal - va? Mi sen - to mo - rir! ohi-mè! ohi-mè! mi sen - to mo - rir!
Who, who will save him? I feel death approach, ah me! ah me! I feel death approach!
ppp
morendo
col canto
Ramphis. (In the crypt.)
tonante
Ra-da - mès! Ra-da - mès! Ra-da - mès!
Ra-da - mès! Ra-da - mès! Ra-da - mès! (from the crypt.)

senza misura
Tu ri - ve - la - sti del - la patria i se - gre - ti al - lo stra - nie - ro.— Di -
Thou hast betray - ed of thy count - ry the secrets to aid the foe - man.— De -
Amneris.
Allegro.
Ah pie -
Mer - cy!
a tempo
con impeto
scol - pa - ti!
fend thy - self!
E - gli - ta - ce: Tra - di - tor!
He is si - lent. Traitor vile!
Chorus.
Di - scol - pa - ti!
De - fend thy - self!
Tra - di - tor!
Trai - tor vile!
Allegro. (♩= 120.)
pp
ff
tà!— e - gli è in - no - cen - te, Nu - mi,— pie -
spare him, ne'er was he guilt - y; ah,— spare him,—
p
tà,— Nu - mi,— piè - tà!
heaven, ah,— spare his— life.
Ramphis.
Ra - da -
Ra - da -
(in the subterranean hall.)

mès!__ Ra-da - mès!__ Ra-da - mès!__
mès!__ Ra-da - mès!__ Ra-da - mès!__
ff
senza misura
Tu di-ser-ta-sti dal cam-po il di che pre-ce-dea la pu - gna.__ Di-
Thou hast desert-ed th'en-campment the very day before the com - bat.__ De-
Amneris.
con impeto
Ah pie-
Mer-cy,
scol-pa-ti!
fend thy-self!
Egli ta-ce:__ Tra-di-tor!
He is si-lent. Trai-tor vile!
Chorus.
Di-scol-pa-ti!
De-fend thy-self!
Tra-di-tor!
Trai-tor vile!
Di-scol-pa-ti!
De-fend thy-self!
Tra-di-tor!
Trai-tor vile!
ppp
ff
tà!__ ah!__ lo sal - va - te, Nu - mi,__ pie - -
spare him, save_ him, oh heav'n_ ah,__ spare him,_
p
dim.

tà, Nu - mi, pie - tà!
heav'n, ah, spare his life!
Ramphis.
(from the crypt)
ff
Ra - da - mès! Ra - da - mès! Ra - da - mès!
Ra - da - mes! Ra - da - mes! Ra - da - mes!
ff
senza misura
tua fè vio - la - sti, al - la pa - tria sper - giu - ro, al Re, al - l'o - nor. Di - scol - pa - ti!
Hast broken faith as a trai - tor to country, to King, to hon - or. De - fend thyself!
Amneris.
Ah pie -
Mer - cy
E - gli ta - ce: Tra - di - tor!
He is si - lent. Trai - tor vile!
Chorus.
Di - scol - pa - ti! Tra - di - tor!
De - fend thy - self! Trai - tor vile!
ppp
ff

tà! Ah! lo sal - va - te, Nu - mi, pie - tà, Nu - mi, pie -
spare him! Save him, oh heav - en, ah heav'n, spare him, heav'n, spare his
dim.
Poco ritenuto.
tà!
life!
Ramphis.
Ra - da - mès, è de - ci - so il tuo
Ra - da - mès, we thy fate have de -
Chorus.
Ra - da - mès, è de - ci - so il tuo
Ra - da - mès, we thy fate have de -
Ra - da - mès, è de - ci - so il tuo
Ra - da - mès, we thy fate have de -
Poco ritenuto.
fa - to, de - gli in - fa - mi la mor - te tu a -
cid - ed, of a trai - tor the fate shall be
fa - to; de - gli in - fa - mi la mor - te tu a -
cid - ed, of a trai - tor the fate shall be
fa - to; de - gli in - fa - mi la mor - te tu a -
cid - ed, of a trai - tor the fate shall be

vrai; sot - to l'a - ra del Nu - me sde - gna - - to, sot - to
thine; 'Neath the al - tar whose god thou'st de - rid - - ed, 'neath the
vrai; sot - to l'a - ra del Nu - me sde - gna - to, sot - to
thine; 'Neath the al - tar whose god thou'st de - rid - - ed, 'neath the
vrai; sot - to l'a - ra del Nu - me sde - gna - - to, sot - to
thine; 'Neath the al - tar whose god thou'st de - rid - - ed, 'neath the
ff
l'a - ra del Nu - me sde - gna - to a te vi - vo fia schiu - so l'a - vel.
al - tar whose god thou hast de - rid - ed, Thou a sepulchre liv - ing shalt find.
l'a - ra del Nu - me sde - gna - to a te vi - vo fia schiuso l'a - vel.
al - tar whose god thou hast de - rid - ed, Thou a sep - ul - chre liv - ing shalt find.
l'a - ra del Nu - me sde - gna - to a te vi - vo fia schiuso l'a - vel.
al - tar whose god thou hast de - rid - ed, Thou a - sep - ul - chre liv - ing shalt find.
Più vivo.
ff string.
ff

Amneris.
A lui vi - vo- la tom-ba- oh! gl'in - fa-mi! nè di
Find a sep - ul-chre liv-ing- Oh, ye wretches! ev-er
dim.
pp
san-gue son pa-ghi giam - mai- e si chia-man mi - ni - stri del
blood-thirsty, vengeful, and blind, Yet who serve of kind heav-en the
Come prima.
(The Priests re-enter out of the crypt)
ciel!
shrine!
ff
Ramphis.
Tra - di - tor! tra - di - tor! tra - di -
Trai - tor vile! trai - tor vile! trai - tor
Chorus.
Tra - di - tor! tra - di - tor! tra - di -
Trai - tor vile! trai - tor vile! trai - tor
Tra - di - tor! tra - di - tor! tra - di -
Trai - tor vile! trai - tor vile! trai - tor
pp

Amneris. (confronting the Priests.)
molto accentato.
Sa - cer - do - - ti: com - pi - ste un de - lit - to! Ti - gri in - fa - mi di sangue as - se -
Priests of I - sis, your sentence is o - dious! Ti - gers, ev - er ex - ult - ing in
tor!
vile!
tor!
vile!
tor!
vile!
Lo stesso movimento.
col canto
a tempo, affrett.
ta - te - voi la ter - ra ed i Nu - mi ol - trag -
slaugh - ter! Of the earth and the gods all laws ye
Poco mosso. (♩ = 120.)
m. s.
gia - te! voi pu - ni - to chi col - pe non
out - rage! He is guilt - less, whose death ye de -

Amneris.
(to Ramphis)
ha! Sa-cer-do - te: que-st'uo-mo che uc-
vise! Priest of I - sis, this man whom you
Ramphis.
È tra-di - tor! mor - rà!
He is con-demn'd! He dies!
Chorus.
È tra-di - tor! mor - rà!
He is con-demn'd! He dies!
È tra-di - tor! mor - rà!
He is con-demn'd! He dies!
ff
f
ci - di, tu - lo sai - da me un gior - no fu a - ma - to - L'a - na - te - ma d'un
mur-der, Well ye know, in my heart I have cher - ish'd: May the curse of a
ppp
m.s.
co - re stra - - zia - to col suo
heart whose hope has per - - ish'd - Fall on
ff

Amneris.
san-gue su te ri-ca - drà!
him— who mer-cy de - nies!
Ramphis.
È tra-di-tor! mor-
He is con-demn'd! He
Chorus.
È tra-di - tor! mor-
He is con - demn'd! He
È tra-di - tor! mor-
He is con - demn'd! He
ff
Sostenuto.
frase larga
Voi— la ter - ra ed i Nu-mi ol-trag - gia -
All— the laws— of the earth and gods ye out -
rà!
dies!
mor-
re -
rà!
dies!
mor-
re -
rà!
dies!
mor-
re -
Sostenuto.
frase larga

te voi pu - ni - te, pu - ni - te chi
rage! He is guilt - less, is guilt - less, whose
rà!
call!
rà!
call!
rà!
call!
Mosso.
col - pe non ha. Ah no, ah no, non è, non
death ye de - vise! Ah no, ah no, not he, not
È tra - di - tor! mor - rà! mor - rà!
A trai - tor's death he dies! He dies!
È tra - di - tor! mor - rà! mor - rà!
A trai - tor's death he dies! He dies!
È tra - di - tor! mor - rà! mor - rà!
A trai - tor's death he dies! He dies!
Mosso. (♩ = 160)

stent.
è, ah no, non è, no, no, non è tra - di -
he, ah no, ah no, no, no, no trai - tor is
È tra - di - tor! è tra - di - tor! mor -
He is con - demn'd! He is con - demn'd! He
È tra - di - tor! è tra - di - tor! mor -
He is con - demn'd! He is con - demn'd! He
È tra - di - tor! è tra - di - tor! mor -
He is con - demn'd! He is con - demn'd! He
stent.
tor, ah no, ah no, non è tra - di - tor, ah no, ah no,
he, ah no, ah no, no trai - tor is he, ah no, ah no,
ff
rà! è tra - di - tor! mor - rà, mor - rà! è tra - di -
dies! He is con - demn'd! He dies, he dies! He is con -
ff
rà! è tra - di - tor! mor - rà, mor - rà! è tra - di -
dies! He is con - demn'd! He dies, he dies! He is con -
ff
rà! è tra - di - tor! mor - rà, mor - rà! è tra - di -
dies! He is con - demn'd! He dies, he dies! He is con -
ff

non è tra - di - tor - pie - tà! pie - ta! pie - ta! pie - ta!
no trai - - tor is he, ah spare! ah spare! ah spare! ah spare!
tor! mor - rà, mor - rà! è tra - di - tor! mor - rà, mor-
demn'd! He dies, he dies! He is con-demn'd! He dies, he
tor! mor - rà, mor - rà! è tra - di - tor! mor - rà, mor-
demn'd! He dies, he dies! He is con-demn'd! He dies, he
tor! mor - rà, mor - rà! è tra - di - tor! mor - rà, mor-
demn'd! He dies, he dies! He is con-demn'd! He dies, he
p
dim. sempre
(Exeunt Ramphis and Priests)
rà! Tra - di - tor!
dies! Ay, he dies!
rà! Tra - di - tor!
dies! Ay, he dies!
rà! Tra - di - tor!
dies! Ay, he dies!
pp

tra - di - tor!
He shall die!
tra - di -
He shall
Amneris.
Em - pia raz - za! a - na - te - ma su
Im - pious priest - hood! curs - es light on ye
tor!
die!
ff
voi! la ven - det - ta del ciel, del ciel— scen - de -
all! On your heads heav - en's ven - geance, ven - geance will

(exit wildly)
rà! a - na - te- -ma su voi!
fall! curs - es light on ye all!
fff
tutta forza
fz
fz
fz
fz
fz
fz
tr
secca

Scene and Duet. Last Finale.

Aïda and Radamès _ Amneris and Chorus.

SCENE II. The scene is divided into two floors. The upper floor represents the interior of the Temple of Vulcan, resplendent with gold and glittering light. The lower floor is a crypt. Long arcades vanishing in the gloom. Colossal statues of Osiris with crossed hands support the pillars of the vault. Radamès is discovered in the crypt, on the steps of the stairs leading into the vault. Above, two priests are in the act of letting down the stone which closes the subterranean apartment.

dolcissimo
A - i - da, o - ve sei tu? Pos - sa tu al - me - no vi - ver fe -
A - i - da, where now art thou? What-e'er be - fall me, may'st thou be
pp
li - ce e la mia sor - te or - ren - da sem - pre i - gno - rar! Qual
hap - py, ne'er may my fright - ful doom reach thy gen - tle ear. What
ge - mi - to! U - na lar - va u - na vi -
groan was that! 'Tis a phantom some vi - sion
pp
sion No! for - ma u - ma - na è
dread No! sure that form is
que - sta Ciel! A -
hu - man! Heav'n! A -

Aïda.
Son i - o!
'Tis I, love!
(in the utmost despair)
i - da!
i - da!
Tu? in que - sta tom - ba?
Thou? with me here bu - ried?
Andante. (♩ = 63)
Aïda. (sadly.)
Pre - sa - go il co - re del - la tua con - danna, in questa tom - ba che per te s'a -
My heart for - bod - ed this thy dread - ful sentence, And to this tomb, that shuts on thee its
ppp
pri - va io pe - ne - trai fur - ti - va.... e qui lon - ta - na da o - gni u - ma - no
por - tal, I crept un - seen by mor - tal. Here, far from all, where none can more be -
con passione
dolce largo
allarg.
morendo
sguardo nel - le tue braccia de - si - ai mo - ri - re.
hold us, clasp'd in thy arms I am re - solv'd to per - ish.
Radamès.
con passione
Poco meno.
Mo - rir!... sì pu - ra e
To die!... so pure and
Poco meno. (♩ = 60)
pp
pp
espressivo.

pp
bel - la! mo - rir! per me d'a - mo - re... de - gli an - ni tuoi nel
love - ly! For me thy - self so doom - ing... In all thy beau - ty
dolciss. senza string.
fio - re, de - gl'an - ni tuoi nel fio - re fu - gir la vi - - - -
bloom - ing, in all thy beau - ty bloom - ing Fade thus for ev - - -
ta! T'a - vea il cie - lo per l'a - mor cre - a - ta, ed io tuc -
er! Thou whom the heav'ns a - lone for love cre - at - ed, But to des -
con espressione
dim.
con grazia dolciss. e legato
ci - do per a - ver - ti a - ma - ta! No, non mor - rai! trop - po t'a - mai! trop - po sei bel -
troy thee was my love then fat - ed! Ah, no, those eyes so clear I prize, for death too love - ly

Aïda.
(as in a trance)
Andantino.
dolciss.
Ve - di?- di mor-te l'an-ge-lo
Seest thou, where death, in an-gel-guise,
là!
are!
Andantino. (♩ = 80)
pp
radian - te a noi s'ap - pres - sa
In heav'n-ly ra-diance beam-ing,
ne ad - du-ce a e - ter-ni gau - dii
Would waft us to e-ter-nal joys,
sov-ra i suoi van-ni d'or.
On golden wings a - bove?
Già veggo il ciel di-schiuder - si
See, heaven's gates are o-pen wide,
dolce
ppp
i - vi o-gni af-fan-no ces - sa,
Where tears are nev-er stream - ing,
dim.
i - vi co - min-cia l'e-sta-si
Where on-ly joy and bliss a-bide,

dolciss.
d'un im-mor-ta-le a-mor, co-min-cia l'e-sta-si d'un
And nev-er-fad-ing love, Where joy and bliss a-bide, And
dolciss.
rall.
Lo stesso movimento.
im-mor-ta-le a-mor.
nev-er-fad-ing love.
Chorus in the Temple.
Priestesses.
SOPRANO.
mf
Im - men-so, im-men-so
Al - migh-ty, al-migh-ty
TENOR.
mf
Ah!
Ah!
Priests.
BASSES.
mf
Ah!
Ah!
Lo stesso movimento. (♩= 80)
col canto

Tri-ste can-to!
Doleful chanting!
Il no-stro in - no di
It is our death-chant re-
Il tri-pu - dio dei sacerdoti.
Of the priests 'tis the in-vo-cation.
Fthà, del mon - - - - do spi-ri-to a - ni - ma-
Phthà, that wak - - - - est, in all things breathing
mor-te.
sounding.
(trying to displace the stone closing the vault)
Nè le mie for-ti brac-cia smuo-ve-re ti po-tran - no, o fa-tal
Can-not my lus-ty sin-ews move from its place a mo-ment this fa-tal
tor,
life,
noi t'in-vo-
lo! we in-
noi t'in-vo-
lo! we in-
noi t'in-vo-
lo! we in-
ff
ppp

In-van!
In vain!
Tut - to è fi-
All, all is
pie-tra!
stone!
chia - - - mo, t'in - - vo-
voke thee, we in-
pp
p
tr
dim.
ni-to sul-la ter-ra per noi.
o-ver, hope on earth have we none.
(with sad resignation)
È ve-ro! è ve-ro!
I fear it! I fear it!
Meno mosso.
O terra ad-
Fare-well, oh
chiam, t'in - - vo - chiam.
voke, we in - voke.
Meno mosso.(♩ = 60)

ten.
f
pp
morendo
di-o; ad-di - o val-le di pian-ti,_ so-gno di gau-dio che in do-lor_ sva-
earth, fare-well thou vale of sor-row, Brief dream of joy con-demn'd to end_ in
ppp
nì_ A noi si schiu-de, si schiu-de il ciel,_ si schiu-de il
woe; To us now o-pens, now o-pens the sky,_ now opens the
ciel e l'al-me er-ran - ti_ vo-la-no al rag-gio dell' e-ter-no
sky, an end-less mor - row_ Un-shad-ow'd there e-ter-nal-ly shall
dolciss.
dì.
glow.
O ter-ra ad-di-o;
Farewell, oh earth,
Radamès.
O ter-ra ad-di-o; ad-di-o val-le di pian-ti,_ so-gno di
Farewell, oh earth, fare-well, thou vale_ of sor-row_ Brief dream of

a noi si schiu - de,
To us now o - pens,
gau - dio che in do - lor sva - nì, a noi si
joy con - demn'd to end in woe, To us now
si schiu - de il ciel,
now opes the sky,
schiu - de, si schiu - de il ciel, si schiu - de il
o - pens, now o - pens the sky, now opes the
si schiude il ciel, a noi si schiude il
now opes the sky, to us now opes the
ciel e l'al-me er-ran - ti vo-lano al rag - gio dell' e - ter - no
sky, an end-less mor - row Un-shad-ow'd there e - ter-nal - ly shall

Come prima
ciel.
sky.
dì.
glow.
SOPRANO.
Chorus.
Im - men - so Fthà, noi t'in - vo - chiam, noi t'in - vo -
Al - might - y Phthà, thee we in - voke, thee we in -
TENOR.
Im - men - so Fthà, noi t'in - vo - chiam, noi t'in - vo -
Al - might - y Phthà, thee we in - voke, thee we in -
BASS.
Come prima
Ah! si schiu -
Ah! now o -
Ah! si schiu -
Ah! now o -
chiam, t'in - vo - chiam,
voke, we in - voke,
chiam,
voke,
chiam, t'in - vo - chiam,
voke, we in - voke,
ppp
rinf.
f
pp
dim.

pp
Come prima.
de il ciel. O ter - ra ad -
pens the sky. Fare - well, oh
Amneris (appears habited in mourning, and throws herself on the stone closing the vault.)
pp
de il ciel. O ter - ra ad -
pens the sky. Fare - well, oh
t'in - vo - chiam!
we in - voke!
t'in - vo - chiam!
we in - voke!
f
ppp
Come prima. (♩=62.)
pp
di - o, ad - di - o val - le di pian - ti, so - gno di
earth, fare - well, thou vale of sor - row, Brief dream of
(suffocated with emotion.)
Pa - ce t'implo - ro.
Peace ev - er - last - ing.
pp
di - o, ad - di - o val - le di pian - ti, so - gno di
earth, fare - well, thou vale of sor - row, Brief dream of
pppp
f
ppp

gaudio che in do-lor sva-nì, a noi si schiude, si schiu-de il
joy condemn'd to end in woe; To us now o-pens, now o-pens the
sal-ma a-do-ra-ta,
Oh, my belov-ed,
gaudio che in do-lor sva-nì, a noi si schiude, si schiu-de il
joy condemn'd to end in woe; To us now o-pens, now o-pens the
pppp
un poco cresc.
ciel, si schiude il ciel e l'alme erran - ti vo-la-no al
sky, now opes the sky, an end-less mor - row Unshadow'd
I-si pla-ca-ta, I - si pla -
I-sis re-lenting, I - sis re -
ciel, si schiude il ciel e l'alme erran - ti vo-la-no al
sky, now opes the sky, an end-less mor - row Unshadow'd
ppp

dolciss.
pp
rag - gio del-l'e-ter-no dì,— il ciel,— il ciel,—
there e - ter-nal-ly shall glow,— the sky,— the sky,
ca - ta ti schiu - da il ciel!
lent-ing greet thee on high!
rag - gio del-l'e-ter-no dì,— il ciel,— il
there e - ter-nal-ly shall glow,— the sky,— the
Chorus.
p
Noi t'in - vochiam, noi t'in - vochiam,
Thee we in - voke, thee we in - voke,
f
ppp
sempre dolciss.
si schiude il ciel, si schiude il
now opes the sky, now opes the
ciel,— si schiude il ciel, si schiude il
sky,— now opes the sky, now opes the
im - men - so Fthà, im - men - so Fthà!
al - might - y Phthà, al - might - y Phthà!

(falls and dies in the arms of Radamès.)
ciel.
sky.
Amneris.
ancora più piano
Pa - ce t'implo - ro,
Peace ev - er - last - ing,
pa - ce t'implo - ro,
peace ev - er - lasting,
ciel.
sky.
(Curtain slowly descends.)
ppp
Amneris.
pa-ce, pa-ce,
ev-er - lasting
pa - - - ce!
peace!
Im - men - so Fthà!
Al - might - y Phthà!
Im - men - so Fthà!
Al - might - y Phthà!
8
pppp

End of Opera.

CPSIA information can be obtained
at www.ICGtesting.com
Printed in the USA
BVHW061103310321
603809BV00004B/271

9 781376 178760